The World of Louisa May Alcott

A first-time glimpse into the life and times of Louisa May Alcott, author of *Little Women*

William Anderson

with photographs by David Wade

HarperPerennial

A Division of HarperCollinsPublishers

JB
Alcott

All color photography of natural settings, landmarks, and artifacts in this book is the work of David Wade. European photo research was conducted by Yumiko Taniguchi and Michael Voss. Historical photographs, documents, and ephemera are from the collections of the following organizations, whose courtesy is acknowledged with thanks:

Louisa May Alcott Memorial Association: pages 9, 10, 11 (upper left only), 31 (upper left), 44 (both lower right), 45 (upper right), 47 (lower right), 48, 50, 51, 52 (upper right), 55, 56, 60, 64, 69, 71, 86, 88, 90, 91, 94, 95, 97, 99, 100, 101, 103 (ticket), 104, 106 (upper right), 107, 109, 110, 111, 112.

Minuteman National Historical Park: page 27 (diagrams).

Concord Free Public Library: pages 29, 52 (upper left), 56 (upper left), 58, 61, 78, 84, 94 (manuscript page), 96 (lower left), 106 (upper and lower left), 108 (lower left).

Norman Rockwell Museum and Norman Rockwell Family Trust: pages 82 and 83.

Culver Pictures: page 72.

Bettmann Archive: page 14.

Anonymous Source: page 54.

An edition of this book was published in Japan in 1992 by Kyuryudo Art Publishing Company Ltd.

HarperCollins books may be purchased for educational, business, or sales promotional use. For information please write: Special Markets Department, HarperCollins Publishers, Inc., 10 East 53rd Street, New York, NY 10022.

FIRST EDITION

Maps by Tsuyoshi Matsumoto

ISBN 0-06-095156-7

01 10 9 8 7 6 5 4 3 2

Contents

Louisa May Alcott: Renaissance Woman

Louisa May Alcott became America's premier author of children's books during the late nineteenth century with lively, fresh tales about the daily experiences of young people. The most famous of these books, *Little Women*, loosely based on Louisa's own family life, still remains one of the world's most beloved novels. *Little Women* is filled with both good humor and pathos, and a generous dash of the author's own practical common sense. In her own life and in her written words, Louisa May Alcott recognized the value of work and duty and constant personal improvement.

The words, thoughts, and philosophy of her large oeuvre mirror the personage of Louisa May Alcott: career woman, writer, reformer, and suffragist. *Little Women*'s chief character, Jo March, served as the spokesperson for Louisa and her real-life beliefs. More than a century after Jo March first spoke from the pages of *Little Women*, she is still dispensing her no-nonsense, sometimes impetuous, creativity and self-reliance to new readers.

In addition to *Little Women*, Louisa's March family trilogy included *Little Men* and *Jo's Boys*. These books also mirror the author's family life. Though Louisa's sisters, Anna, Elizabeth, and May, became Meg, Beth, and Amy in their fictional forms, their stories are rooted in fact. "Facts in the stories are true, though often changed as to time and place," Louisa explained after her books were successfully launched and readers wondered when the facts ceased and the fiction began.

The beginnings of Louisa May Alcott's literary life were rooted in a childhood surrounded by the vibrant intellectual movement in New England known as Transcendentalism. Louisa's father, Amos Bronson Alcott, was a significant figure in this philosophical movement.

Growing up during the 1830s and 1840s in Boston and Concord, Massachusetts, Louisa learned to know and love writers and thinkers, including Ralph Waldo Emerson and Henry David Thoreau. At home she was instructed to cultivate and write down her own thoughts and dreams, as well as to be conscious of the needs of others. In an era of rigidly stratified social and ethnic groups, the Alcotts gave of themselves generously to the poor, to immigrants, and to blacks. In a culture that relegated women to the kitchen or the parlor and found interest in women's rights an odious trait, Louisa May Alcott staunchly asserted her independence and served as a role model to more conventional females of her generation.

As a New Englander, Louisa May Alcott was Yankee in character, strongly conventional in much of her lifestyle. She was also an unconventional Victorian woman, notably independent as she took a broad view of the world around her. Her zest for adventure and her self-assurance took her far from the domestic home life she portrayed in *Little Women*.

As a young girl, Louisa ventured from the family circle to earn a living and to make her mark as a writer. Her fighting patriotism during the Civil War sought its own battlefield when she served as a Union nurse in Washington. Her thirst for culture and travel took her to Europe twice. When fame as an author was achieved, she was a welcome if occasional figure among the literati of Boston and New York. In literary circles she was the distinguished Miss Alcott, whose work was eagerly awaited by editors and handsomely paid by publishers.

The writings that emanated from the Alcott homes in Concord and Boston became entertainment for generations, read and loved around the globe.

And now let's step into the world of Louisa May Alcott.

Louisa May Alcott

A Life of Words

In addition to her many books, Louisa May Alcott left behind the legacy of her letters and journals. Writing was her compulsive trait, a habit as much as an outlet. Louisa's conversations with herself and with others in her world poured out in a steady stream of words, chronicling nearly fifty years of her life.

As early as 1850, when she was seventeen, Louisa valued the introspection and wisdom she gained from her periodic journals. "Must always try to think of the willful, moody girl I try to manage," she wrote of herself. "In my journal I write of her to see how she gets on. If I look into the glass, I try to keep down vanity about my long hair, my well-shaped head, and my good nose. My quick tongue is always getting me into trouble, and my moodiness makes it hard to be cheerful, when I think . . . how much worry it is to live and how many things I long to do. . . .

"I can't talk to anyone but Mother about my troubles," Louisa wrote of her youthful internal struggles. The bond between Louisa and her mother, Abba May Alcott, was a strong one. Equally important was the influence of her philosopher father, Amos Bronson Alcott. He delighted in her journal writing and offered his own solutions to the dilemmas she sometimes discussed on paper.

Together, Abba and Bronson created an extraordinary atmosphere in which to nurture their daughter.

"Among my hills and woods I had fine free times alone. . . ."

Louisa May Alcott posed for a daguerreotype in the 1850s. "Miss Alcott's appearance was striking and impressive, rather than beautiful. Her figure was tall and well-proportioned, indicating strength. . . ." (Ednah Dow Cheney)

Bronson

Amos Bronson Alcott was born on November 29, 1799, to a Connecticut farming family. In his rural surroundings he developed a thirst for education and reading and a vibrant curiosity for the world beyond the Connecticut hills. In 1818 he left on the first of his five peddler's trips, selling goods in the southern states, where isolated plantations welcomed goods and news from the North.

Bronson's true calling was not merchandising; it was teaching. He was innovative and unusual in his methods, his theories based on the elevation of the child's mind, the development of individual curiosity, and the realization of the link between man and nature. His first teaching post was in Cheshire, Connecticut. Like most of his future schools, the Cheshire School was a mix of great success and controversy over the idealist Alcott's unfamiliar methods.

Carolyn Hildreth painted Bronson Alcott when he was in his early fifties.

Bronson Alcott spent part of his boyhood in this home near the summit of Spindle Hill, Wolcott, Connecticut.

Bronson, who liked to sketch as well as write, drew from memory his Spindle Hill home.

After closing his Cheshire School in June 1827, Bronson went to visit Reverend Samuel J. May in Brooklyn, Connecticut. The minister had heard of Alcott's inspired teaching and wanted to meet him. While visiting the Reverend May, Bronson also met the Reverend's sister, Abigail.

The May family of Boston was a distinguished one. Abba, as she was called, was born in 1800, the youngest child of Colonel and Mrs. Joseph May. Colonel May was a prominent member of King's Chapel, Boston, and dedicated to good works and philanthropy among the city's poor and needy. His example instilled the same sense of duty to the less fortunate in his daughter, Abba.

The Mays arranged for a teaching position for Bronson in Boston's Infant School in 1828. Two years later, on May 23, 1830, Bronson Alcott and Abba May were married at King's Chapel.

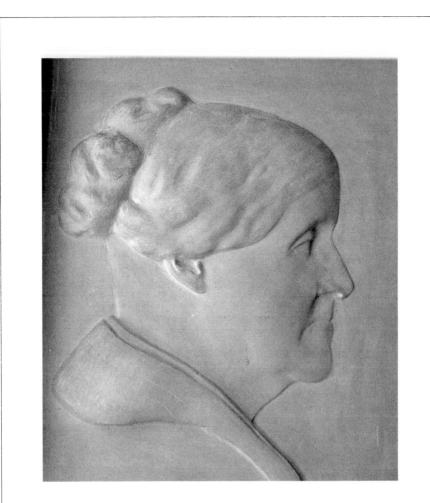

A bas-relief portrait of Abba May Alcott.

Abba Alcott's distinguished lineage included Aunt Hancock, a great-aunt whose first husband was John Hancock. The Hancock mansion in Boston was built in 1737.

King's Chapel in Boston still stands at the corner of Tremont and School streets. A tablet honoring Colonel May was placed inside in 1874.

Germantown, 1831–1834

Soon after the Alcotts were married, wealthy Quakers from Philadelphia offered to sponsor a school for Bronson to teach. Bronson's published essay, "On the Principles and Methods of Infant Instruction," had attracted the attention of the Quakers.

Bronson opened a primary school connected with the Germantown Academy. The Alcotts moved into Pine Place, a cottage provided by the school. Some of the students boarded with the Alcotts, which intensified Bronson's influence over the children.

At Pine Place on March 16, 1831, the Alcotts' first child was born: Anna Bronson. "Joy, gratitude, hope and affection were all mingled in our feelings," Bronson wrote. He immediately began to keep detailed records on his daughter's life as he watched her grow and develop physically and mentally. It was a process he continued with zest for two more Alcott babies.

On Bronson's thirty-third birthday, a second daughter was born to the Alcotts. The date was November 29, 1832; the child was named Louisa May. Bronson wrote to his mother that she was "a very fine, fat little creature, much larger than Anna was at her birth."

After teaching his classes and recording the incidents of his girls' development, Bronson also read widely, improving what he felt was his own incomplete education. He delved into the works of Coleridge, Plato, Thomas Carlyle, and especially savored the educational theories of the Swiss reformer, Pestalozzi.

The death of one of the sponsors of Bronson's school resulted in its decline, until only a few students remained. Bronson considered teaching to be his "noble work." He was despondent when he entered his schoolroom and "no little prattlers welcomed my presence. It was tenantless and unswept."

There was no choice but to return to Boston. In the summer of 1834 Bronson, Abba, Anna, and Louisa moved back to Boston, nearly penniless. What awaited them was Bronson's greatest achievement and his greatest failure as a teacher: the Temple School.

Boston, 1834

The golden dome of the State House in Boston overlooks the grassy Common. The building was constructed in 1798.

Boston was always Bronson's great consolation. There were bookstores and libraries and people ready to listen to him and his philosophical ideas. For Abba, Boston was home, and she had many relatives, friends, and supporters there. Not all of them approved of her improvident husband, but many were ready to help Abba with gifts of money, clothes, and food to ease the lives of her family.

When the Alcotts returned to Boston, they found it to be in a boom. Industry made the city one of America's manufacturing centers. Railroads were a new development. The city streets were lit by gas. Boston Common, America's oldest public park, stretched along the western edge of the downtown district.

Among Boston's wealthy and intellectual population were people willing to listen to Bronson Alcott's progressive educational ideas. With the assistance of one of his followers, Elizabeth Palmer Peabody, enough students were found to establish a new school. It was called the Temple School, because it occupied rooms in the newly built Masonic Temple.

On September 22, 1834, the Temple School opened. Bronson's assistant was Elizabeth Peabody.

Boston Common was a favorite spot of young Louisa and still serves as a popular park in the city's downtown area.

While the Alcotts moved in the refined intellectual circles of Boston, the city teemed with business and economic growth. The Quincy Market was a busy spot where goods from the seaport and wharf district were sold to citizens of the city.

Bronson taught his students with a conversational method, and Elizabeth Peabody recorded and transcribed the dialogues. Bronson, who believed in the Transcendental theory that children possessed tabulae rasae (blank slates), was thrilled with the responses children made to his questions. A sampling of them was recorded when Elizabeth Peabody published *The Record of a School*.

Bronson made sure that the Temple School was filled with beauty and color and comfort; he hated the thought of the drafty, uncomfortable, ugly schools he had attended as a boy. He spent his own meager salary on adornments for the school. While he excelled at conversation sessions with students, he left the teaching of Latin and arithmetic to Miss Peabody. Other subjects stressed were geography, drawing, writing, individual reading, and spelling. The keeping of personal journals was encouraged; this was an activity much encouraged by Transcendentalists like Bronson. The reading of his favorite book, *The Pilgrim's Progress*, was also a trademark of the school.

Throughout 1836, the Temple School flourished. At the end of the year Bronson published *Conversations on the Gospels*, a book detailing more of his probing question-and-answer sessions with his young scholars. The book, which Bronson hoped would finally give him wide acceptance as a revolutionary educator, did just the opposite. Conservative ministers, editors, and prominent Bostonians labeled *Conversations* as dangerously radical.

Pupils dropped out of the Temple School. It moved to smaller quarters. The last blow came when Bronson admitted a black student. Support dwindled, and in 1839, the school shut down.

Once again, Bronson Alcott was without a school, and he was also deep in debt.

Birth of Elizabeth, 1835

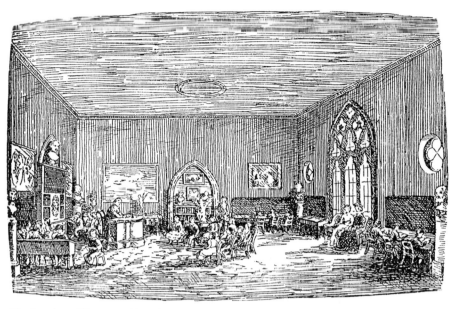

The interior of Bronson Alcott's Temple School.

During the Boston years, Anna and Louisa grew very close to their mother while Bronson was busy with his teaching, reading, and writing. Abba was a protective, supportive mother and her bond with Louisa was especially strong. "You and I always liked to be grouped together," Abba noted in a message to her daughter.

Louisa became an active child in contrast to the gentle, docile Anna. More than once Louisa's roaming spirit led her to run away, which she said was "one of the delights of my childhood."

The Alcott girls became three when Elizabeth Sewall was born in June of 1835. She was the namesake of Bronson's Temple School assistant, but became known as Beth or Lizzie.

St. Paul's Church and the Boston Masonic Temple.

The Alcotts encouraged their young children to keep journals and carry on correspondence. The journals were open for their parents to read and respond to. Birthdays were occasions for Bronson to write to his daughters and comment on their growth and character development.

Concord, 1840

An early photo of the Dove Cote.

The Alcotts soon became acquainted with Concord's naturalist, Henry David Thoreau. Thoreau cherished his solitary walks through the Concord countryside, searching for Indian relics and examples of flora and fauna. But occasionally he allowed company, including the Alcott and Emerson children.

Henry Thoreau and his brother John kept a school called the Concord Academy, which in many ways was similar to the Temple School. Anna and Louisa Alcott were among the Thoreau brothers' enthusiastic students. Most memorable were the brothers' field trips with their classes around Concord.

The Dove Cote was the birthplace of the last Alcott child.

With the failure of the Temple School, the demands of creditors, and the need for a home they could afford, the Alcotts left Boston. Friendship between Bronson and Ralph Waldo Emerson had deepened and Concord's philosopher urged the Alcotts to move close to him. Emerson so admired Bronson's thoughts that he advised him to stop teaching and pursue writing.

In the spring of 1840, the Alcotts moved to Concord. They rented a cottage near the South Bridge from Edmund Hosmer for fifty-two dollars a year. It became known as the Dove Cote because Louisa later used its setting as Meg's first married home in *Little Women*.

The beauty of the countryside and the quiet village life of Concord appealed to the Alcotts. Louisa recalled their first Concord days as "the happiest of my life." The Alcott girls merged into a group of playmates including the Emerson children. Louisa was often a leader, organizing pranks, plays, and games.

During the Alcotts' interlude in Concord, the fourth and last daughter of the family was born. Abigail May was born on July 16, 1840, and named for her mother. She was later nicknamed Abby and eventually called May.

The Thoreau brothers' school.

The Monadnock Mountains, as seen from Harvard, Massachusetts.

Bronson's 1835 meeting with essayist Ralph Waldo Emerson soon led to contacts with other Transcendentalists. The writings and thoughts of this varied group of thinking men and women were so significant that the era became known as the Flowering of New England.

The Transcendentalists rejected the Puritan theology which seemed to them to deny man's creative and spiritual vibrance. They believed that all men had access to God, and linked man, nature, and God in spiritual unity.

Emerson explained that basic truths of the universe were acquired by an intuition that "never reasons, never proves, it simply perceives." The beliefs of the Transcendentalists translated into a variety of lifestyles. For the first time in history, women were accepted and valued as intellectual equals of men. Transcendentalists were ardent abolitionists. Reforms in dress, diet, and society were welcomed and experimentation was encouraged. Bronson's educational theories were a direct result of his philosophical leanings.

While Bronson became increasingly engrossed with his philosopher friends, journals, and self-cultivation, the Alcott family lived sim-

ply. Bronson occasionally worked at day labor, but often food was scarce for the growing family. There were long stretches of eating only vegetables and apples washed down with cold water. Bronson was a vegetarian; part of his philosophical code prohibited him from robbing any animal in the Universe of its flesh.

In 1842 British reformers invited Bronson to visit England. His ideas on education were more popular in England than they were in America, so much so that a school, Alcott House, was named in his honor. For six months Bronson toured schools, met with British Transcendentalists, and planned what he called a New Eden.

When Bronson returned to his family in October 1842, he was not alone. With him were two English friends with plans to begin a communal experiment to be called the consociate family.

A site was selected for the emerging group, one hundred acres of farm land near Harvard, Massachusetts, which was about fifteen miles from Concord. On June 1, 1843, the Alcotts arrived at Fruitlands.

The center for the Transcendental communal experiment was a drafty red farmhouse. It housed the Alcott family and several permanent and visiting participants in the New Eden. The present day Fruitlands Museums was founded by Clara Endicott Sears.

Fruitlands today celebrates the Transcendental and Shaker influence on American thought and culture.

Bronson Alcott's beloved apples thrive at Fruitlands.

"The divine man," Bronson wrote, "dwells amidst gardens and orchards, a grower of plants and fruits."

Life in the Fruitlands farmhouse was devoted to simple living and self-improvement.

Ralph Waldo Emerson visited Fruitlands in its summer splendor. "They look well in July," he noted. "We will see them in December." He doubted that Fruitlands would succeed.

Twelve-year-old Anna Alcott described Fruitlands' beauty: "It is a beautiful place surrounded by hills, green fields and woods, and Still River is at some distance flowing quietly along. Wachusett and Monadnock Mountains are in sight, and also some houses and fields of grain."

The Alcotts, Charles Lane and his son William, and the several other participants in the consociate family lived by a set of reformer's rules. Mr. Lane designed linen garments for each member of the group. Cotton was not used because it was produced by slave labor; wool was also unacceptable because it stole the cloak of sheep.

A strict vegetarian diet was the fare at Fruitlands. "No animal substances tempt us," noted Charles Lane. "Our sole beverage is pure fountain water." The Alcotts were used to a diet of bread, fruit, and vegetables because Bronson had long believed it to be sinful to sacrifice animals for human consumption.

The Fruitlands men planted gardens and crops, but were often away trying to bring new converts to the experimental commune. Most of the work of the house and the extended family was performed by Abba Alcott. She grew irritated at all the rules designed to create ideal lives, and she was exhausted from worry and labor. "I hope the experiment will not bereave me of my mind," she wrote.

At harvest time, Bronson Alcott and Charles Lane went to New York to describe their experimental commune to all who would listen. While they were gone, the barley crop was threatened by a storm, so the Alcott girls and William Lane worked together gathering the crop into Abba's white sheets. It was a small harvest, and Abba predicted an even scantier diet than they were then eating.

The older Alcott girls, Anna and Louisa, were disturbed by their mother's worries, their father's preoccupation with his failing commune, and the annoyances of living in a small house with others. There was talk of the Fruitlanders joining a nearby Shaker community, which did not allow a family unit and stressed a separation of the sexes. "I was very unhappy," Louisa wrote. "Anna and I cried in bed and I prayed to keep us all together."

Late in the fall of 1843, the situation at Fruitlands became intolerable. Food and wood were lacking and it was evident that Bronson Alcott's high-minded experiment was a failure. He collapsed in depression and misery. Abba took charge and arranged for the departure from Fruitlands.

In January 1844, the Alcotts moved to nearby Still River. They rented rooms for fifty cents a week. The girls attended school again and Abba Alcott plotted and planned for money to support the family. Bronson believed that it was wrong to hire out his body for labor. He was wholly absorbed in his spiritual elevation.

Abba and Bronson Alcott's bedroom in the Fruitlands farmhouse was a quiet haven in the overcrowded shelter for the consociate family.

Bronson Alcott believed that the extended family at Fruitlands could awaken heightened spirit in each other. Sharing ideas, virtues, and lifestyles would achieve this goal.

Despite the intense intellectual and philosophical atmosphere at Fruitlands, the Alcott children had enjoyable days. "It was good fun," Louisa wrote of husking corn in the barn.

With varied ideas, conflicting opinions, and no official leader, Fruitlands remained a dream that Bronson could not transform into reality.

Louisa turned eleven as the Fruitlands experiment was coming to a close. On November 29, 1843, she wrote in her journal: "It was Father's and my birthday. We had some nice presents. We played in the snow before school. Mother read *Rosamond* when we sewed. Father asked us in the eve what fault troubled us most. I said my bad temper."

A visitor at Fruitlands inquired whether the commune used any beasts of burden. Abba Alcott replied bitterly: "Only one woman!"

Lessons were not neglected while the Alcotts were at Fruitlands. The girls were tutored and encouraged in their journal writing, reading, and letter exchanges. Charles Lane, whom Louisa found annoying, did most of the teaching. Another visitor at Fruitlands, Miss Page, taught music.

Louisa's journal records the virtues she wished to possess: Patience, Obedience, Industry, Love, Generosity, Respect, Silence, Perseverance, Self-denial. She claimed she hoped to rid herself of Idleness, Impatience, Selfishness, Wilfulness, Impudence, Activity, Vanity, Pride, and the Love of Cats.

Abba Alcott kindly guided Louisa in her struggles against ill-temper and anger; she saw many similarities between herself and her second daughter. "I felt sad because I have been cross today, and did not mind Mother," Louisa wrote in her journal. Abba wrote notes of encouragement. "Keep quiet," she advised, "read, walk, but do not talk much till all is peace again."

Despite the fireplaces in the Fruitlands house, the place was cold and drafty.

Still River, 1844

Louisa loved to run through the Massachusetts countryside. "I always thought I must have been a deer or a horse in some former state, because it was such a joy to run," she wrote.

When the Alcotts settled in Still River, Bronson tended nearly an acre of garden plot.

Wrote Bronson: "The garden is the tie uniting man and nature."

"Gardening," Bronson declared, "is blending man's genius with natural substance."

"I had an early run in the woods before the dew was off the grass," Louisa wrote in her journal. "I sang for joy, my heart was so bright and the world so beautiful."

After the Fruitlands failure the Alcotts slowly settled into Still River life. The girls attended Miss Chase's school and made friends. At Brick Ends they invented little plays and performed them. Louisa was a leader, often organizing the children into theatricals and contests. In the Brick Ends woodshed, a mock wedding was arranged for Louisa and a boy named Walter Gardner. She wore an apron for a veil.

Bronson still thought of creating a communal family of Transcendental people, but could not find participants. He and Abba investigated idealistic communities in New England, but could find none to suit them. Finally they decided to return to Concord.

In the fall of 1844, the Alcotts once again packed their possessions and returned to the town where Bronson was happiest. They settled in with the Edmund Hosmer family for the winter and then searched for a home of their own.

The Alcotts moved to Brick Ends in Still River in April 1844. It was a wooden house with brick walls on either end. The rent of twenty-five dollars a year included the necessary garden plot to provide summer food for the family.

The Concord River.

Hillside, 1845

The Wayside, called Hillside by the Alcotts.

Experiences at Hillside with her sisters Anna, Beth, and May provided incidents used in *Little Women*.

A The original colonial house built in the early 1700s.

B The Alcott additions of 1845–1846.

C Nathaniel Hawthorne's extensive renovations in 1860.

D Author Margaret Sidney's alterations.

Colonel May, Abba's father, died and one thousand dollars became available for the Alcotts from his estate. Ralph Waldo Emerson added five hundred dollars and the Alcotts bought a farmhouse on Lexington Road in Concord. The place was called Hillside and it was just a mile from Emerson's home. On April 1, 1845, the Alcotts moved in.

Bronson Alcott, who was a creative carpenter, immediately began to revamp the 130-year-old Colonial house. He added rooms and fashioned a summer kitchen at the rear of the house. On the acreage, he created elaborate gardens and a screened spot for the family's cold water showers.

One of Louisa's wishes was a room of her own in the Hillside house where she could read, write, and think. In March 1846, when she was thirteen, she wrote in her journal: "I have at last got the little room I have wanted so long, and am very happy about it. It does me good to be alone, and Mother has made it very pretty and neat for me. My work-basket and desk are by the window and my closet is full of dried herbs that smell very nice. The door that opens into the garden will be very pretty in summer, and I can run off to the woods when I like."

Louisa recalled the Hillside days as the happiest of her childhood. She was mindful of her parents' financial struggles, and resolved then to help her family, a role she continued for the rest of her life.

While at Hillside Louisa entered into what she called her sentimental period. At fifteen, she began dreaming of her future, seriously writing poetry, romances and an introspective journal.

Her father often sat with Ralph Waldo Emerson in his book-lined study up the road from Hillside. Bronson and Emerson inspired one another and their exchange of ideas was a constant philosophical stimulus. Louisa, too, was welcome at the Emerson home and borrowed freely from the library there.

Louisa was deeply inspired by the German novelist, poet, and playwright, Johann von Goethe. Goethe's *Faust* and other writings made him a central figure in German Romantic literature. In the Emerson library she discovered a book called *Goethe's Correspondence with a Child*. She was immediately enamored with the idea of making Emerson her Goethe and being his youthful follower. "So I wrote letters to him, but was wise enough never to send them, left wild flowers on the doorstep of my 'Master' . . . and was fond of wandering by moonlight, or sitting in a cherry tree at midnight till the owls scared me to bed."

Bronson Alcott's 1845 sketch of the family home in Concord, Hillside.

Emerson's study, a refuge for Bronson and other philosophers and a lending library for Louisa.

Goethe

Goethe (1749–1832) became one of Europe's most celebrated writers in the early 1800s. Louisa called him "my favorite author." His *Faust* dealt with a man who continually sought his own perfection, which is a goal closely attuned to Transcendental philosophy. Louisa, many years later, reworked this theme in her anonymous novel, *A Modern Mephistopheles*.

Emerson

Ralph Waldo Emerson (1803–1882) gained wide acclaim as a forceful and original philosopher with works like "Nature" and "Representative Men" and essays including "The American Scholar" and "The Over-Soul." He was a constant supporter, friend, and adviser to the Alcotts. Wrote Louisa: "Emerson remained my beloved 'Master' while he lived, doing more for me . . . than he ever knew, by the simple beauty of his life, the truth and wisdom of his books. . . ."

Recollections of
My Childhood
by
Lousia May Alcott

One of my earliest memories is of playing with books in my father's study. Building towers and bridges of the big dictionaries, looking at pictures, pretending to read, and scribbling on blank pages whenever pen or pencil could be found. Many of these first attempts at authorship still exist, and I often wonder if these childish plays did not influence my after life, since books have been my greatest comfort, castle-building a never-failing delight, and scribbling a very profitable amusement.

My mother always declared that I was an abolitionist at the age of three. During the Garrison riot in Boston the portrait of George Thompson was hidden under a bed in our house for safe-keeping, and I am told that I used to go and comfort "the good man who helped poor slaves" in his captivity. However that may be, the conversion was genuine, and my greatest pride is in the fact that I have lived to know the brave men and women who did so much for the cause, and that I had a very small share in the war which put an end to a great wrong.

Being born on the birthday of Columbus I seem to have something of my patron saint's spirit of adventure, and running away was one of the delights of my childhood. Many a social lunch have I shared with hospitable Irish beggar children, as we ate our crusts, cold potatoes and salt fish on voyages of discovery among the ash heaps of the waste lands that then lay where the Albany station now stands.

Many an impromptu picnic have I had on the dear old Common, with strange boys, pretty babies and friendly dogs, who always seemed to feel that this reckless young person needed looking after.

On one occasion the town-crier found me fast asleep at nine o'clock at night, on a door-step in Bedford Street, with my head pillowed on the curly breast of a big Newfoundland, who was with difficulty persuaded to release the weary little wanderer who had sobbed herself to sleep there.

I often smile as I pass that door, and never forget to give a grateful pat to every big dog I meet, for never have I slept more soundly than on that dusty step, nor found a better friend than the noble animal who watched over the lost baby so faithfully.

My father's school was the only one I ever went to, and when this was broken up because he introduced methods now all the fashion, our lessons went on at home, for he was always sure of four little pupils who firmly believed in their teacher, though they have not done him all the credit he deserved.

I never liked arithmetic or grammar, and dodged these branches on all occasions; but reading, composition, history and geography I enjoyed, as well as the stories read to us with a skill which made the dullest charming and useful.

"Pilgrim's Progress," Krummacher's "Parables," Miss Edgeworth, and the best of the dear old fairy tales make that hour the pleasantest of our day. On Sundays we had a simple service of Bible stories, hymns, and conversations about the state of our little consciences and the conduct of our childish lives which never will be forgotten.

Walks each morning round the Common while in the city, and long tramps over hill and dale when our home was in the country, were a part of our education, as well as every sort of housework, for which I have always been very grateful, since such knowledge makes one independent in these days of domestic tribulations with the help who are too often only hindrances.

Needle-work began early, and at ten my skillful sister made a linen shirt beautifully, while at twelve I set up as a doll's dress-maker, with my sign out, and wonderful models in my window. All the children employed me, and my turbans were the rage at one time to the great dismay of the neighbors' hens, who were hotly hunted down, that I might tweak out their downiest feathers to adorn the dolls' head-gear.

Active exercise was my delight from the time when a child of six I drove my hoop round the Common without stopping, to the days when I did my twenty miles in five hours and went to a party in the evening.

I always thought I must have been a deer or a horse in some former state, because it was such a joy to run. No boy could be my friend till I had beaten him in a race, and no girl if she refused to climb trees, leap fences and be a tomboy.

My wise mother, anxious to give me a strong body to support a lively brain, turned me loose in the country and let me run wild, learning of nature what no books can teach, and being led, as those who truly love her seldom fail to be, "Through nature up to nature's God."

I remember running over the hills just at dawn one summer morning, and pausing to rest in the silent woods saw, through an arch of trees, the sun rise over river, hill and wide green meadows as I never saw it before.

Something born of the lovely hour, a happy mood, and the unfolding aspirations of a child's soul seemed to bring me very near to God, and in the hush of that morning hour I always felt that I "got religion" as the phrase goes. A new and vital sense of His presence, tender and sustaining as a father's arms, came to me then, never to change through forty years of life's vicissitudes, but to grow stronger for the sharp discipline of poverty and pain, sorrow and success.

Those Concord days were the happiest of my life, for we had charming playmates in the little Emersons, Channings, Hawthornes and Goodwins, with the illustrious parents and their friends to enjoy our pranks and share our excursions.

Plays in the barn were a favorite amusement, and we dramatized the fairy tales in great style. Our giant came tumbling off a loft when Jack cut down the squash vine running up a ladder to represent the immortal bean. Cinderella rolled away in a vast pumpkin, and a long, black pudding was lowered by invisible hands to fasten itself on the nose of the woman who wasted her three wishes.

Little pilgrims journeyed over the hills with scrip and staff and cockle-shells in their hats; elves held their pretty revels among the pines, and "Peter Wilkins" flying ladies came swinging down on the birch tree-tops. Lords and ladies haunted the garden, and mermaids splashed in the bath-house of woven willows over the brook.

People wondered at our frolics, but enjoyed them, and droll stories are still told of the adventures of those days. Mr. Emerson and Margaret Fuller were visiting my parents one afternoon, and the conversation having turned to the ever interesting subject of education, Miss Fuller said:

"Well, Mr. Alcott, you have been able to carry out your methods in your own family, and I should like to see your model children."

She did in a few moments, for as the guests stood on the door steps a wild uproar approached, and round the corner of the house came a wheelbarrow holding baby May arrayed as a queen; I was the horse, bitted and bridled and driven by my elder sister Anna, while Lizzie played dog and barked as loud as her gentle voice permitted.

All were shouting and wild with fun which, however, came to a sudden end as we espied the stately group before us, for my foot tripped, and down we all went in a laughing heap, while my mother put a climax to the joke by saying with a dramatic wave of the hand:

"Here are the model children, Miss Fuller."

My sentimental period began at fifteen when I fell to writing romances, poems, a "heart journal," and dreaming dreams of a splendid future.

Browsing over Mr. Emerson's library I found "Goethe's Correspondence with a Child," and was at once fired with the desire to be a second Bettine, making my father's friend my

Goethe. So I wrote letters to him, but was wise enough never to send them, left wild flowers on the door-steps of my "Master," sung Mignon's song in very bad German under his window, and was fond of wandering by moonlight, or sitting in a cherry-tree at midnight till the owls scared me to bed.

The girlish folly did not last long, and the letters were burnt years ago, but Goethe is still my favorite author, and Emerson remained my beloved "Master" while he lived, doing more for me, as for many another young soul, than he ever knew, by the simple beauty of his life, the truth and wisdom of his books, the example of a good, great man untempted and unspoiled by the world which he made nobler while in it, and left the richer when he went.

The trials of life began about this time, and my happy childhood ended. Money is never plentiful in a philosopher's house, and even the maternal pelican could not supply all our wants on the small income which was freely shared with every needy soul who asked for help.

Fugitive slaves were sheltered under our roof, and my first pupil was a very black George Washington whom I taught to write on the hearth with charcoal, his big fingers finding pen and pencil unmanageable.

Motherless girls seeking protection were guarded among us; hungry travelers sent on to our door to be fed and warmed, and if the philosopher happened to own two coats the best went to a needy brother, for these were practical Christians who had the most perfect faith in Providence, and never found it betrayed.

In those days the prophets were not honored in their own land, and Concord had not yet discovered her great men. It was a sort of refuge for reformers of all sorts whom the good natives regarded as lunatics, harmless but amusing.

My father went away to hold his classes and conversations, and we women folk began to feel that we also might do something. So one gloomy November day we decided to move to Boston and try our fate again after years in the wilderness.

My father's prospect was as promising as a philosopher's ever is in a money-making world, my mother's friends offered her a good salary as their missionary to the poor, and my sister and I hoped to teach. It was an anxious council, and always preferring action to discussion, I took a brisk run over the hill and then settled down for "a good think" in my favorite retreat.

It was an old cart-wheel, half hidden in grass under the locusts where I used to sit to wrestle with my sums, and usually forget them scribbling verses or fairy tales on my slate instead. Perched on the hub I surveyed the prospect and found it rather gloomy, with leafless trees, sere grass, leaden sky and frosty air, but the hopeful heart of fifteen beat warmly under the old red shawl, visions of success gave the gray clouds a silver lining, and I said defiantly, as I shook my fist at fate embodied in a crow cawing dismally on the fence nearby,—

"I *will* do something by-and-by. Don't care what, teach, sew, act, write, anything to help the family; and I'll be rich and famous and happy before I die, see if I won't!"

Startled by this audacious outburst the crow flew away, but the old wheel creaked as if it began to turn at that moment, stirred by the intense desire of an ambitious girl to work for those she loved and find some reward when the duty was done.

I did not mind the omen then, and returned to the house cold but resolute. I think I began to shoulder my burden then and there, for when the free country life ended the wild colt soon learned to tug in harness, only breaking loose now and then for a taste of beloved liberty.

My sisters and I had cherished fine dreams of a home in the city, but when we found ourselves in a small house at the South End with not a tree in sight, only a back yard to play in, and no money to buy any of the splendors before us, we all rebelled and longed for the country again.

Anna soon found little pupils, and trudged away each morning to her daily task, pausing at the corner to wave her hand to me in answer to my salute with the duster. My father went to his classes at his room down town, mother to her all-absorbing poor, the little girls to school, and I was left to keep house, feeling like a caged sea-gull as I washed dishes and cooked in the basement kitchen where my prospect was limited to a procession of muddy boots.

Good drill, but very hard, and my only consolation was the evening reunion when all met with such varied reports of the day's adventures, we could not fail to find both amusement and instruction.

Father brought news from the upper world, and the wise, good people who adorned it; mother, usually much dilapidated because she *would* give away her clothes, with sad tales of suffering and sin from the darker side of life; gentle Anna a modest account of her success as teacher, for even at seventeen her sweet nature won all who knew her, and her patience quelled the most rebellious pupil.

My reports were usually a mixture of the tragic and the comic, and the children poured their small joys and woes into the family bosom where comfort and sympathy were always to be found.

Then we youngsters adjourned to the kitchen for our fun, which usually consisted of writing, dressing and acting a series of remarkable plays. In one I remember I took five parts and Anna four, with lightning changes of costume, and characters varying from a Greek prince in silver armor to a murderer in chains.

It was good training for memory and fingers, for we recited pages without a fault, and made every sort of property from a harp to a fairy's spangled wings. Later we acted Shakespeare, and Hamlet was my favorite hero, played with a gloomy glare and a tragic stalk which I have never seen surpassed.

But we were now beginning to play our parts on a real stage, and to know something of the pathetic side of life with its hard facts, irksome duties, many temptations and the daily sacrifice of self. Fortunately we had the truest, tenderest of guides and guards, and so learned the sweet uses of adversity, the value of honest work, the beautiful law of compensation which gives more than it takes, and the real significance of life.

At sixteen I began to teach twenty pupils, and for ten years learned to know and love children. The story writing went on all the while with the usual trials of beginners. Fairy tales told the Emersons made the first printed book, and "Hospital Sketches" the first successful one.

Every experience went into the chauldron to come out as froth, or evaporate in smoke, till time and suffering strengthened and clarified the mixture of truth and fancy, and a wholesome draught for children began to flow pleasantly and profitably.

So the omen proved a true one, and the wheel of fortune turned slowly, till the girl of fifteen found herself a woman of fifty with her prophetic dream beautifully realized, her duty done, her reward far greater than she deserved.

Historic Concord, Home of the Alcotts

The Minuteman, a statue by Daniel Chester French, was dedicated a century after the famous Concord battle.

First Parish Universal Unitarian Church in Concord.

Concord, Massachusetts, has a dual fame: it is steeped in colonial and Revolutionary history and it is known as the home of American authors.

Concord lies nineteen miles northwest of Boston. It was founded by Puritans in 1635. Its meadows, its ponds, the slow-moving Concord and Merrimack Rivers, and its dense forests made it a place of great natural beauty. The earliest settlers encountered a hostile environment for farming, and their necessary independence has persisted in the town's spirit through the ensuing three and a half centuries.

Concord's identity as a New England town is divided into two distinct chapters. The first centers on the town's role in the Revolutionary War. In April 1775 American patriots opposed the forces of the British troops in a battle at Concord's North Bridge. It was, as later resident Ralph Waldo Emerson wrote, "the shot heard round the world." The battle at North Bridge officially opened the American Revolution against the British Crown and its excessive taxation of the colonies.

Sixty years after the American and British engagement at North Bridge, the literary chapter of Concord had its start. In 1834 Ralph Waldo Emerson bought a solid, white frame house along the Cambridge Turnpike, not far from the center of Concord. A one-time Unitarian minister, Emerson distinguished himself as a lecturer, poet, and essayist. His literary reputation and his role in American Transcendentalism brought Concord its first reputation as a literary mecca. Emerson served as a magnet to other writers and thinkers; his charismatic hospitality drew many to Concord, both to visit and to live.

Soon after moving to Concord, Emerson befriended the Harvard graduate Henry David Thoreau. While Emerson had known Concord as a visitor during his boyhood, Thoreau was a native. His love of nature and his almost fierce independent spirit were attuned to the emerging Transcendental philosophy of Emerson. It was on Emerson's land adjoining Walden Pond that Thoreau built a one-room house in which to live a simple life, study nature, and write in solitude.

His book *Walden: Or, Life in the Woods* was the result of his experiment.

Solitary, brooding Nathaniel Hawthorne came to Concord with his new bride, Sophia, in 1842. They lived at the Old Manse, which belonged to the Emerson-Ripley families, until 1845. The idyllic surroundings—close to the Concord River, with meadows and forests nearby—suited the reclusive Hawthorne and his wife. Hawthorne's book *Mosses from an Old Manse* was written during the author's first stay in Concord.

And so Concord became one of America's most important literary gathering places. The lure of Emerson and the Transcendentalists brought a steady stream of thinkers and writers to the pastoral town. Among those who drew inspiration and encouragement from the Sage of Concord were Margaret Fuller, William Ellery Channing, Bret Harte, Walt Whitman, Henry Wadsworth Longfellow, and Henry James.

"His books are surcharged with vigorous thoughts, a sprightly wit," said Bronson Alcott of Emerson. "Poet and moralist, he has beauty and truth for all men's edification and delight. His works are studies."

Pre–Civil War and wartime during the 1860s were exciting days in Concord, with most of the community staunchly supporting abolitionist causes and the northern troops. Young Louisa May Alcott served as a Union Army nurse in 1863. Two years after the war, in 1867, the Soldier's Monument was erected in the town square to honor those who died.

Each year on April 19, Patriot's Day is celebrated in Concord. It commemorates the battle between American patriots and British troops in Concord.

The Concord River, wrote Henry David Thoreau, "is remarkable for the gentleness of its current, which is hardly perceptible." Thoreau had a special boat landing in Concord, and invited specially selected friends on excursions. Boating and picnicking along the Concord was a popular pastime for the Emerson, Hawthorne and Alcott children. Louisa May Alcott wrote of one such excursion in the chapter "Camp Laurence" from *Little Women*.

"Tents, lunch, and croquet utensils having been sent on beforehand, the party was soon embarked, and the two boats pushed off together. . . . Laurie and Jo rowed one boat; Mr. Brooke and Ned the other. . . ."

The present bridge across the Concord is a higher, more substantial version than was known in earlier centuries.

Boston, 1848

The Alcotts knew the narrow streets of Boston well.

Bronson Alcott could not find a teaching position in Concord; the town did not accept his methods. So in 1848, hoping to find earning opportunities, the Alcott family left Concord and moved to Boston. Abba Alcott was offered a salary to serve as a "missionary to the poor" in Boston. Louisa and Anna decided to teach.

In Boston the Alcotts settled into a small house on Dedham Street. Bronson rented rooms where he held philosophical "conversations" with small groups of interested persons. His proceeds were skimpy, but as Louisa later said, "he continued to hope."

Abba Alcott became one of the first social workers in America. Boston was crowded with impoverished Irish immigrants, wandering vagrants, unwanted children, and poor families. With support from a group of wealthy patrons, Abba visited the poor, helped find them work, and distributed charity, Bibles, and religious tracts.

Louisa and Anna operated a small school. The younger girls, Beth, twelve, and Abby May, eight, went to school. Sixteen-year-old Louisa called their Boston lives "Good drill, but very hard, and my only consolation was the evening reunion when all met with such varied reports of the day's adventures." For entertainment, the Alcott girls wrote, staged, and costumed fantastic plays. At seventeen, Louisa showed significant leanings to a writing career. She published a family newspaper called the *Olive Leaf.* Her play-scripts, performed by the Alcott girls, included titles like "The Moorish Maiden's Vow," "Bandit's Bride," and "The Captive of Castile." Louisa, in addition to writing, developed a passionate desire to act on the stage, which was shared by Anna.

20 Pinckney Street was the Alcott home in 1854.

In 1852 Louisa sold her first published story for five dollars.

Although Boston was an intellectual and publishing center in America, the city suffered from overcrowding and social problems during the era the Alcotts lived there. By 1849 more than 50,000 Irish immigrants lived there. Abba Alcott's relief work made the entire family mindful of those less fortunate than themselves. Louisa also recalled the city's wealthier neighborhoods and rich shopping areas and her frustration of having "no money to buy the splendors before us."

Flower Fables, 1854

An illustration for *Flower Fables*.

As a teen, Louisa declared that her pen would make her rich and famous. Her early stories appeared in the *Saturday Evening Gazette*. She used a pseudonym, Flora Fairfield, and she called her work great "rubbish." The small sums she earned encouraged Louisa, even though Boston publisher James Fields told her, "You can't write." He advised her to "Stick to your teaching."

In 1854, when she was twenty-two, Louisa's first book was published. She received twenty-two dollars for the publication of *Flower Fables*, a collection of stories she had written when she was sixteen for Ellen Emerson.

The Alcotts found living in Boston too expensive and though Emerson established a fund for the family, there wasn't enough to pay their expenses. At the suggestion of relatives, they decided to move to Walpole, New Hampshire. In July 1855 the family settled in a cottage in the village. Walpole was quiet, but there was an Amateur Dramatic Company. Louisa and Anna enthusiastically participated in the productions of *The Jacobite* and *The Two Bonnycastles*. Anna particularly loved the stage, but her impaired hearing prevented her from pursuing a professional career.

Life in Walpole was often dull and confining for Louisa. Alone, she returned to Boston to sew, to plan stories, and to write for a living. It was a pattern she followed for years to come: time in the shelter of the family circle with interludes of "paddling her own canoe" in bustling Boston.

Death of Beth, 1858

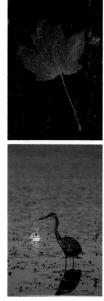

A bout with scarlet fever permanently weakened the third Alcott daughter, Elizabeth. Her prolonged illness concerned the family during their preparations to return to Concord. Beth's decline was wrenching; she would not eat and seldom left her bedroom. On a physician's advice, Abba took her to the seashore but there were no improvements in her condition. Louisa, who showed talent at nursing, often tended her ailing sister. The months dragged on, and Louisa confided to her journal: "A hard thing to bear, but if she is only to suffer, I pray she may go soon."

While Beth slowly wasted away, Bronson looked over and finally selected a home for the family. He bought an acreage with apple trees along the Lexington Road, next door to the family's old Hillside property. The house dated to the late seventeenth century and was in ramshackle repair; most people thought it was worthless. But Bronson Alcott was an early day preservationist and recycler. The home, called Orchard House, had potential and charm and Bronson intended to renovate it into a philosopher's domain.

In October 1857 the Alcotts returned to Concord. They lived in rented quarters while their new home was prepared. Emerson had contributed five hundred dollars to the purchase, and other friends donated money to establish a permanent home for the "Pathetic Family," as Louisa called them.

In March 1858, before the Alcotts could occupy Orchard House, Beth complained that her sewing needle was too heavy for her. She gave away her possessions, and asked that the family gather around. On March 14, 1858, she died at the age of twenty-three. Beth was buried at Sleepy Hollow cemetery in Concord.

"Death never seemed terrible to me," Louisa wrote, "and now is beautiful; so I cannot fear it, but find it friendly and wonderful."

Concord beckoned the Alcotts once more when the charity of their Walpole benefactors waned. Bronson was convinced that they should return to Concord; some of his friends were discussing the establishment of a philosophical college there. "I can do more for you, and for myself, from the Concord position," he explained to Abba. A move to Concord, Abba feared, would be another variation on the old problem of providing an income for the family.

Orchard House

" 'Tis a pretty retreat," Bronson said of Orchard House, "and *ours*; a family mansion to take pride in." His skill as a house planner reflected his literary tastes, but the effect was more successful than his abstruse writing. Bronson enlarged windows in the colonial building, joined a tenant house to the rear, and lowered floors to raise the ceilings. He built bookshelves and created niches for classical busts left over from the Temple School. Adjoining his library and study, a studio was arranged for May's artwork.

The twelve-room Orchard House was painted and papered throughout by the girls. May was encouraged to paint artwork on wall panels throughout the spacious rooms. Bronson's own artistic bent greeted visitors without: his curving rustic fence drew snickers from some Concordians but seemed appropriate with the backdrop of the brown house and tall trees.

The social reformer and Alcott friend, Lydia Maria Child, came to visit and wrote: "The house of the Alcotts took my fancy greatly. Mr. Alcott has architectural taste. . . . He let every old rafter and beam stay in its place, changed old ovens and ash-holes into Saxon-arched alcoves. . . . The result is a house full of queer nooks and corners, and all manner of juttings-out."

For the first time in their married life, Bronson and Abba Alcott were permanently settled in a house that belonged to them.

Wrote Bronson: "My neighbors flatter me in telling me that I have one of the best placed and most picturesque houses in town."

"Much company to see the new house," Louisa wrote. "We won't move again for twenty years if I can help it."

May Alcott, a budding artist, painted Orchard House after the family settled there in 1858.

The Alcotts posed in front of Orchard House during the 1860s; by that time the place was known for its hospitality around Concord. The girls performed theatricals for guests on their usual Monday evening open houses. Abba served homely treats from the kitchen like gingerbread and a dish called apple slump. Bronson engaged anyone who would listen in philosophical conversation. There was singing, games of charades and storytelling. "The Orchard House was filled with smiling faces and happy voices," Julian Hawthorne recalled.

Bronson's beloved apples grew on the Orchard House property, providing fruit for cider, pies and munching. Louisa's nickname for the place became Apple Slump.

Bronson constructed a rustic summer house in the yard; he and May posed there for a photographer.

May's sketch of one corner of Orchard House included her own second-floor bedroom window.

May's work steadily improved during the Orchard House years. Concord provided her with many pastoral scenes.

Family portaits hang in the Orchard House parlor, along with artwork created by May. The piano is believed to be a gift to the Alcott girls from their grandfather Colonel May. The parlor sofa included Louisa's "mood pillow." When it stood on end, she was in a good mood; when it lay flat, she expected the family to avoid her and respect her need for solitude.

Beth's melodeon still stands at the foot of the back stairway.

Little Women tells of Beth's piano, a gift from kindly neighbor Mr. Laurence.

In the dining room of Orchard House, the Alcott girls staged their plays.

Bronson posed in his study, where he read, wrote, and conversed with his famous friends.

After settling in Orchard House Bronson started receiving respect in Concord for his educational ideas.

Bronson

Louisa called the year 1860 the Year of Good Luck mainly because her father was appointed Superintendent of Schools in Concord. He received a small salary. At the age of sixty, he finally received credit for his many talents in the educational field. He visited all the Concord schools and became a well-loved figure. Many of his ideas about learning have become a part of modern education. He encouraged art education, field trips, physical training, nature study, school newspapers, photography study, music, and dance. He frowned on textbooks, believing that individualized reading was more significant.

Bronson's many maxims expressed his theories. Among them was: "To teach, treating students with uniform familiarity, and patience and with the greatest kindness, tenderness and respect."

The hallway at Orchard House.

Bronson's study was off the front hallway at Orchard House.

A photo of Bronson's mother adorned the mantelpiece and May painted a motto on the fireplace in her father's study.

Bronson's novel teaching methods were evident in the story of Mr. March and Demi in *Little Women*. Grandfather and grandson formed the letter W by extending their legs upward.

Abba

In addition to being a capable mother, home-maker and sometime breadwinner for her family, Abba Alcott was a strong reformer. She was one of the "Fighting Mays," whose ancestors had fought against the British in the American Revolution. The Mays were known for their charitable work throughout Boston and were staunch abolitionists. She passionately believed in voting rights for women, in the freeing of slaves, and in her idealistic, philosopher husband.

On one of Bronson's early lecture tours he returned home late one night, tired, hungry, and with one dollar in profit to show his family. "I shall never forget how beautifully mother answered him," Louisa recalled. "With a beaming face she kissed him, saying, 'I call that doing *very well*. Since you are safely home, dear, we don't ask anything more.'"

Abba's philosopher-husband constantly tested her faith through their poverty years. One winter day when the Alcott wood supply was low, a neighbor came asking to borrow wood. Abba thought of her family first, but Bronson assured her that Providence always provided. Wood would come or the weather would warm. He told the neighbor to take away the remaining wood. Not long after, another knock was heard on the door. A man arrived, asking if the Alcotts would take a big load of firewood. They could pay for it later. Bronson reminded Abba: "I said the wood would come or the weather would moderate!"

Louisa paid tribute to her mother in *Little Women*, with her loving characterization of Mrs. March. When asked if her characters were based on real people, Louisa replied that they were. "Mrs. March," she said, "is all true, only not half good enough."

Abba Alcott took a rare rest in her husband's study at Orchard House. As a philosopher's wife, Abba tended to the material needs of the family while her husband explored the metaphysical.

In *Little Women*, Louisa used her own mother as Marmee, who has become one of the most beloved mother figures in literature.

Louisa longed to create a quiet haven for her work-worn mother.

Abba and Bronson's bedroom in Orchard House.

When she was home at Orchard House, Louisa's second-floor bedroom became her writing study. Here she wrote *Little Women*.

S. M. Alcott.

Louisa's forays into Boston from Concord were for the purpose of earning income for what she called the Alcott Sinking Fund. She saw her earnings as art lessons for May, clothes for her sisters, and comforts for Orchard House. "On my usual hunt for employment," she reported to her journal, "as I am not needed at home and seem to be the only breadwinner just now."

Louisa worked as a servant; sewed for money; taught at schools, and served as a governess. In her leisure hours, she worked at her writing. In 1859, when she was twenty-six, Louisa reported that she was "scribbling foolish stories as usual." Many of her tales were published by the *Saturday Evening Gazette*, which paid her from fifteen to twenty dollars per story. "Mark Field's Mistake" earned her thirty dollars, most of which she sent home to her family. "Love and Self-Love" was printed on the pages of the important *Atlantic Monthly* in 1860. The payment of fifty dollars encouraged Louisa. That year she also started writing her first novel. She called it *Moods* and she worked for four years, writing and rewriting it.

Louisa still loved the world of theater and attended Boston productions when she could afford to. She wrote a farce she called *Nat Bachelor's Pleasure Trip* which was produced at Boston's Howard Atheneum in 1860.

On the half-moon desk between the windows, Louisa worked on poetry, short stories, magazine articles, letter-writing, and her beloved journals.

Louisa constantly planned and worked to earn money for her family's needs, but she did not sell her long hair as Jo did in *Little Women*.

Louisa's bedroom at Orchard House was arranged by relatives who remembered it when the house was restored.

Through lessons and constant practice May's artistic talent increased.

May's painting of the wise owl adorned Louisa's fireplace.

Like Jo of *Little Women*, Louisa "fell into a vortex" when she became enthused over a manuscript. She wrote so rapidly that when her right hand was tired, she changed over to her left. Louisa often overtaxed her mental and physical powers while writing, but she was a robust young woman. Once she walked from Concord to Boston in five hours and declared that the twenty-mile trip left her "not very tired."

May's bedroom at Orchard House was adorned with art-work, which she painted on the walls.

Abba May Alcott, named for her mother, preferred to be called by the more sophisticated-sounding May.

May

As the youngest Alcott, May was indulged and admired. She missed the worst of the Alcotts' poverty and according to Louisa's estimation, always seemed to find benefactors to help her in her artwork and her longing for beauty and good times. Louisa was one of May's staunchest supporters and enjoyed doting on her youngest sister.

"She is so graceful and pretty and loves beauty so much," Louisa wrote to Anna. "It is hard for her to be poor and wear other people's ugly things. You and I have learned not to mind *much* but when I think of her I long to dash out and buy the finest that the limited sum of ten dollars can procure."

May grew into an ambitious young woman whose artistic talent was evident to friends and family. She found many sketching opportunities in the Concord area: Walden Pond, the Concord River, and the quaint colonial buildings were all captured on May's sketch pad. She also painted decorative panels of flowers and birds that were purchased for Concord parlors.

Artistic work led to teaching for May, and she taught art classes both in Concord and Boston. Although dedicated to her talent, May was perhaps the most social of the Alcott girls. She loved attending dances and parties and swimming excursions. Croquet was another passion of hers and she was often seen on the lawn of Orchard House with her mallet and wooden ball.

May's luxurious blond hair and her classic face made her an attractive woman, but like Amy in *Little Women*, she was sometimes petty and vain. Louisa, like Jo, loved her young sister, but was also annoyed by her. In *Little Women*, Amy attempts to straighten her nose by attaching a clothes pin to it.

The children's nursery at Orchard House.

A portrait of Lulu, May's daughter, hangs in the Orchard House nursery.

Anna and John

Among the Alcotts' friends were the Pratts, who had participated in Brook Farm, a similar, but more successful experimental commune than Fruitlands. The son of the house, John, was a pleasant man who shared Anna Alcott's love of acting. Together they had participated in the Concord Dramatic Union, which was the forerunner of the present day Concord Players. They acted together in *The Loan of a Lover* and kept company around Concord. When John asked Anna to marry him, the Alcotts asked her to wait awhile; Beth's recent death was separation enough. Abba approved of Anna's match. She wrote that John was "a man of most unimpeachable character." Bronson also considered John a worthy mate for his oldest daughter. "I think well of him," he wrote, "and doubt not of his power of being the good friend and companion of my good daughter."

Anna, unlike Louisa who claimed "I'd rather be a free spinster," had always dreamed of marriage. "When I used to build castles in the air, a wedding scene always found a place among my pictures."

Anna Bronson Alcott became Meg in *Little Women*.

The first Alcott grandchild was Anna's son, Frederick Alcott Pratt. He was born on March 28, 1863. "We were so glad," Louisa wrote, "that a jolly lad was added to the feminine family."

Anna Alcott and John Pratt were married at Orchard House on May 23, 1860. Louisa described the ceremony in her journal, but confided that "I mourn the loss of my Nan, and am not comforted." Guests danced around the wedding couple on the lawn, and Mr. Emerson kissed Anna. Louisa "thought that honor would make even matrimony endurable."

John Bridge Pratt shared Anna's love for theatricals.

The second Pratt son was born on June 24, 1865. He was named John Sewell Pratt. In their Aunt Weedy's (Louisa's) fiction, the Pratt boys became known as Meg's twins, Daisy and Demi.

Louisa's Friends

Bronson's visits to the Concord schools were exciting days for him and for the students.

During the 1860s, Bronson continued as Superintendent of Schools. His reports suggested innovative practices and reported in detail on his observations of the Concord schools. Annual school festivals were held at the Concord Town Hall. In 1861 the festival was particularly festive. Louisa wrote a song that the children sang. Her father, she wrote, "was in his glory, like a happy shepherd with a large flock of sportive lambs." At the close of the program, Bronson was presented with gifts: a copy of his favorite, *The Pilgrim's Progress*, and George Herbert's *Poems*. They were given by the children, as a token of their love for Mr. Alcott. Bronson finally achieved a measure of respect for his creative and caring dedication to education.

After living in Europe, Nathaniel Hawthorne's family moved next door to Orchard House. They renamed the Alcotts' Hillside as the Wayside. The children, Una, Julian, and Rose, were friendly with May and Louisa.

Alfred Whitman, a student at the Sanborn School, became a close friend of the Alcotts. He was among a group of boys Louisa considered "My Lads." When she wrote *Little Women*, perhaps some of his traits were used in the character of Laurie.

Franklin Sanborn, an admirer of Bronson Alcott, opened a school for boys in Concord.

"Our fields and rivers, brooks and groves . . . have not been undeserving of being celebrated. . . ." —Amos Bronson Alcott

Famous Concordians

The entrance hall in the Old Manse

Concord's Old Manse, one-time residence of both Ralph Waldo Emerson and Nathaniel Hawthorne.

The Old Manse

Closest to North Bridge and full of literary associations is the Old Manse, a gray, gambrel-roofed clapboard house built in 1770 by the Reverend William Emerson, Ralph Waldo's grandfather. Reverend Emerson and his family watched the events on North Bridge transpire; he urged the patriots to seek shelter in his house if necessary.

Ralph Waldo Emerson lived in, and later frequently visited, the Manse; he wrote his first book of essays, *Nature*, in its upstairs study.

A second author who was sheltered under the Manse's broad roof was Nathaniel Hawthorne. From 1842 to 1845 Hawthorne and his bride Sophia resided at the Manse, finding its retired surroundings completely idyllic. The Concord River flowed nearby, grassy meadows extended from the yard, and orchard and trees provided a screen of privacy.

In the same study where Emerson had worked, Hawthorne wrote *Mosses from an Old Manse*. His book is not the only scribbling that endures. On a side window, Sophia Hawthorne etched impromptu messages with her diamond wedding ring; in 1843 she wrote that "Man's accidents are God's purposes." The signatures of both Hawthornes are visible on the glass today.

May Alcott's sketch of the Old Manse.

Emerson House

While Emerson's youth was spent at the Old Manse, his decades as a prominent American philosopher, writer, and lecturer were spent in a square white house set back among the trees from the Lexington Road and Cambridge Turnpike. In this gracious Concord residence Emerson held court with the philosophers and writers who gravitated to him; his library and study, right off the main entrance hall, was obviously the heart of the home.

These placid years were interrupted by a fire in 1872 (a servant set off a blaze while snooping in the attic at two A.M.). The Concord fire department was quickly summoned, and with the help of neighbors, most of the rare books and manuscripts from Emerson's library were saved. Louisa May Alcott capably directed teenage boys in the salvaging while the fire was being doused, but some of Emerson's books were lost and some papers charred.

After the fire, the Emersons lived temporarily at the Old Manse, and then toured Europe. When the philosopher and his wife returned the following year, they were surprised to find that the house had been completely renovated for them by Concord friends.

Essayist and poet Ralph Waldo Emerson.

Emerson House.

May Alcott's sketch of Emerson's home.

Emerson's summer house, built by Bronson Alcott.

"I call this my style of building the 'Sylvan'," said Bronson. The curving tree limbs provided the stair rail in the summer house.

Ralph Waldo Emerson composed the "Concord Hymn" to be sung at the dedication of a monument to the Minuteman on July 4, 1837. The monument, placed near Old North Bridge, quickly became a point of pilgrimage in Concord. The poem was sung at the ceremonies to the tune of "Old Hundredth" ("Praise God from Whom All Blessings Flow").

Concord Hymn

By the rude bridge that arched the flood,
    Their flag to April's breeze unfurled,
Here once the embattled farmers stood
    And fired the shot heard round the world.

The foe long since in silence slept;
    Alike the conqueror silent sleeps;
And Time the ruined bridge has swept
    Down the dark stream which seaward creeps.

On this green bank, by this soft stream,
    We set today a votive stone;
That memory may their deed redeem,
    When, like our sires, our sons are gone.

Spirit, that made those heroes dare
    To die, and leave their children free,
Bid Time and Nature gently spare
    The shaft we raise to them and thee.

Hawthorne (1804–1864)

Salem-born Nathaniel Hawthorne lived in Concord, first as a newlywed at the Old Manse, and then at the Wayside, the house once occupied by the Alcotts and called Hillside by them. In 1852 the already famous author of *The Scarlet Letter* and *The House of the Seven Gables* purchased Hillside from the Alcotts.

"I felt myself, for the first time in my life, at home," Hawthorne said of the only house he ever owned. The Hawthornes' Concord residence was interrupted by a seven-year absence in Europe, where Hawthorne served as an American consul in Liverpool, England, for part of that time. When the Hawthornes returned to Concord in 1860, they discovered that their next-door neighbors were the Alcotts of Orchard House.

Bronson looked forward to a congenial relationship with the celebrated Hawthorne and his family. He was sadly disappointed, for Hawthorne was as silent as Bronson was loquacious.

During the Civil War years, Hawthorne worked on four novels but completed none of them. While he struggled with his literary work, he also continued his lifelong reticence and received few visitors.

The younger members of the Alcott and Hawthorne families saw each other socially, but Nathaniel's death in 1864 led to his family's eventual departure from Concord. By the end of the Hawthorne era, the Wayside had undergone a major transformation. No longer was it a simple colonial farmhouse. The Hawthornes had renovated the house by adding a three-story tower and numerous other alterations.

Hawthorne's vaulted study was artistically decorated by a later resident of the Wayside.

The writing study was sometimes impractical for Hawthorne because of extreme heat in summer and cold during the New England winter.

Hawthorne's red leather chair sat next to the parlor fireplace.

Hawthorne's writing study.

Hawthorne liked to disappear in the woodlands of the Wayside.

Thoreau (1817–1862)

Henry David Thoreau

Concord was the home of Henry David Thoreau, who called the town "the most estimable place in all the world." Thoreau was perhaps the most earthy of all the Transcendentalists. Through his forty-four years, he plied many trades: teacher, pencil manufacturer, surveyor, handyman, lecturer, author, and naturalist.

By the time he graduated from Harvard in 1837, Thoreau was already a close friend and disciple of Emerson, and though Thoreau valued his solitude, he mingled with Hawthorne, the Alcotts, and others in the literary community. He was recognized as the best source of information on Concord's flora and fauna, and his lively nature walks made him popular with the children of the area.

From 1845 to 1847 Thoreau lived companionably close to nature in a one-room house built on land owned by Emerson on the edge of Walden Pond. "I went to the woods to live deliberately," Thoreau explained, "to front only the essential facts of life." In 1854 Thoreau published *Walden*, which related his experiences living near the pond and shared his philosophies with readers. He did not intend that readers imitate his lifestyle, but hoped they would "accept such portions as apply to them."

Research and excavations in 1945 uncovered the original site of the Walden house.

Thoreau's Walden house, built at a cost of "$28. 12½," was moved from the site and not preserved, but Concord visitors may view an exact replica.

Thoreau's birthplace near Concord.

Thoreau's desk, now displayed at
the Fruitlands Museum.

Thoreau's love of independence, his Abolitionist activities, his devotion to nature and his Transcendental writings made him a welcome addition to the Alcott circle of friends. Thoreau surveyed the Orchard House property for them, he attended Anna's wedding, he listened to and appreciated Bronson. "He is the best natured man I ever met," Thoreau said of Bronson Alcott. The Alcott girls regarded Henry Thoreau as a valued friend, mentor, and older brother.

When Thoreau died at forty-four from consumption, Concordians mourned his loss. "We have been accustomed to consider him the salt of things so long that they must lose their savor without his to season them," observed Bronson. Thoreau's death in May 1862 prompted Louisa to write a poem of tribute, which she entitled "Thoreau's Flute." It appeared to great acclaim in *The Atlantic Monthly.*

The Alcotts shared Henry David Thoreau's love of walking through the unspoiled Concord countryside. Wrote Thoreau: "I cannot preserve my health and spirits unless I spend four hours a day at least—and it is commonly more than that—sauntering through the woods and over the hills and fields, absolutely free from all worldly engagements."

Hospital Sketches, 1863

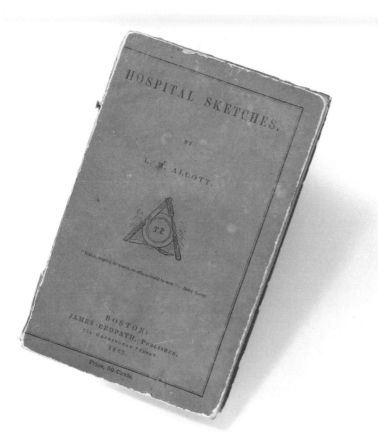

The Alcotts believed that slavery was a great evil, so they followed developments and news of the Civil War when it began in 1861. Louisa longed to do her part for the war effort so she applied for a position as an army nurse. She was thirty when she reported to the Union Hotel Hospital in Washington, D.C., late in 1862.

She nursed the war wounded and comforted the patients, despite the primitive surroundings of the makeshift hospital. Her nursing experience was short; Louisa herself contracted typhoid pneumonia and was very ill. Bronson came to Washington to escort her back to Concord. For weeks she lay near death at Orchard House.

After serving as a Civil War nurse, Louisa's book *Hospital Sketches* was published. As she said, it was "the first successful one."

John Brown's deeds in behalf of the abolitionist movement were highly regarded by the Transcendentalists.

Louisa worked hard in the poor wartime conditions to comfort, heal and care for the sick and wounded soldiers.

Some of Louisa's letters from Union Hospital back home to her family were printed in *Commonwealth.* After Louisa recovered from typhoid, she reworked her letters, changed names and some situations, and produced *Hospital Sketches.* Redpath Publishers printed *Hospital Sketches* as a book. Its characterizations of Louisa's brave patients and its flashes of humor and compassion made the book very popular. One of Louisa's best-loved characters was a dying soldier named John Sulie from Virginia. He died while holding her hand in the hospital.

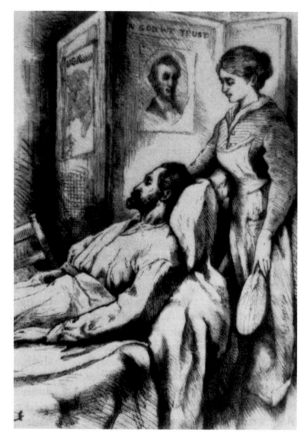

Louisa said that *Hospital Sketches* showed her her writing style.

In 1865 Louisa's novel *Moods* was published; one of the main characters, Adam Warwick, was based on Henry David Thoreau.

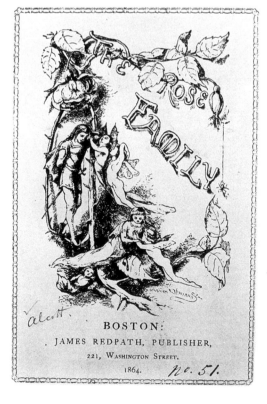

Louisa received fifty dollars for *The Rose Family* when it appeared in 1864.

Louisa's war experience had produced *Hospital Sketches* and a degree of fame, but it had also weakened her health. Use of calomel, which contained mercury, poisoned her system. She battled the aftereffects of the poison the rest of her life.

In 1863 Louisa earned nearly six hundred dollars from writing. She constantly worked on manuscripts that were accepted by an increasing number of important magazines and newspapers. Some of her work was published under the pseudonym A. M. Barnard. Louisa's dramatic, sensa-tional tales were called "blood and thunders." The titles explain themselves; among them are "Pauline's Passion," "The Skeleton in the Closet," and "A Whisper in the Dark."

Louisa's thrillers brought good money. They were published in popular illustrated newspapers like *Frank Leslie's Illustrated Weekly* and *The Flag of Our Union*.

Years after she wrote them, Louisa dismissed her mysteries and thrillers as "romantic rubbish" and "necessity stories."

Louisa's First Tour of Europe, 1865–1866

Boston Harbor.

Like most well-educated New Englanders, Louisa aspired to make a grand tour of Europe. Despite her growing stature as a writer, her fees for stories did not allow her many indulgences other than the satisfaction of keeping the Alcott family afloat in Concord. But in 1865 an opportunity came for Louisa to see Europe as a nurse-companion to a young invalid named Alice Weld.

With family and friends encouraging her to make the journey, Louisa embarked from Boston Harbor in July 1865 for a year of travel. "I could not realize that my long-desired dream was coming true," she wrote. On July 29 Louisa and her companion arrived at Liverpool, England. "I was heartily glad," she observed, "to set my feet on solid earth."

Travels in August and September included journeys through England, Germany, and finally Switzerland. Louisa enthused over the new scenes and stimulating cultural opportunities, but chafed at the restrictions she felt as a paid companion to a fussy semi-invalid.

Highlights from Louisa's travel journal: On the Rhine River: "It was too beautiful to describe, so I shall not try; but I feel richer and better for that memorable day."

On the Alps: "Tall, white, spectral looking shapes they were, towering above the green hills and valleys that lay between."

On Heidelberg, Germany: "A charming old place surrounded by mountains. We went to the Castle and had a fine time roving about the ruins, looking at the view from the great terrace, admiring the quaint stone images of knights, saints, monsters, and angels."

Frankfurt am Main.

1-Boston
2-Liverpool
3-London
4-Dover
5-Ostende
6-Brussels
7-Cologne
8-Koblenz
9-Biebrich
10-Schwalbach
11-Wiesbaden
12-Frankfurt
13 Heidelberg
14-Baden-Baden
15-Freiburg
16-Basel
17-Berne
18-Fribourg
19-Lausanne
20-Vevey
21-Geneva
22-Nice
23-Paris

England

Netherlands

Germany

Poland

Belgium

Seine River

Rhine River

France

Austria

Switzerland

Portugal

Spain

Italy

Louisa enjoyed seeing a favorite author's home, the Goethe house in Wiesbaden.

Statuary in Frankfurt.

From Heidelberg, Louisa and her companion went to Baden-Baden. She wrote, "The old chateau was my delight, and we passed a morning going up and down to visit it. Next to Freiburg, where the Cathedral delighted me extremely, being full of old carved images and designs . . ."

Louisa wrote that Baden-Baden was "a very fashionable place."

Spending winter months in Nice, Louisa remarked on the French city: "very pleasant, climate lovely, and sea beautiful."

In England, Louisa heard her idol, Charles Dickens, perform a reading.

In London, Louisa's sight-seeing included St. Paul's Cathedral *(left),* the Tower of London, Windsor, parks, famous gardens, and historic sites. She loved the spots with literary connections, or as she said, "all manner of haunts of famous men and women." She viewed Milton's home, Thackeray's boyhood locale, and the inn where Dickens wrote *The Pickwick Papers.*

"The view of the lake was lovely," Louisa wrote of Lausanne, "with rocky mountains opposite, little towns at their feet, vineyards along the hillsides, and pretty boats on the lake, the water of which was the loveliest blue."

While in Vevay, Louisa met a young Pole at the pension where she was stopping with her invalid companion. His name was Ladislas Wisniewski. Laddie, as Louisa began calling him, was a Polish revolutionary, on a health cure in Switzerland following months of imprisonment with other Polish patriots.

Louisa was enamored of young Laddie's endearing ways, and in her nurturing way, was soon mothering him. Together they walked, sailed, enjoyed music, and exchanged language lessons. For two months, Laddie was a cheerful part of Louisa's daily adventures. "Sad times for all," she remarked in her journal, when the friends went their separate ways.

In May 1866 Louisa left her role as nurse-companion and traveled independently until she returned to Concord in July. While in Paris she reencountered Laddie. She did not know it then, but the engaging young Pole would soon serve as the model for Laurie in *Little Women.*

Rowing with Laddie helped fill Louisa's days during the sojourn at Vevay.

Little Women, 1868

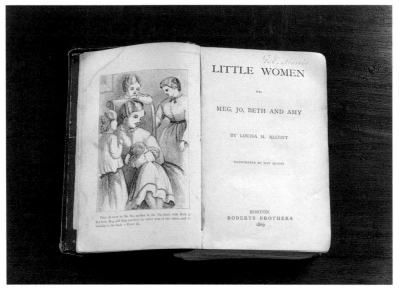

The first edition of *Little Women*.

Louisa once edited *Merry's Museum*.

In 1867 Louisa was asked to become editor of *Merry's Museum: An Illustrated Magazine for Boys and Girls*. The annual five-hundred-dollar salary gave Louisa a steady income and it also allowed her to test her abilities at writing for children. Much of the editing work was done by Louisa while she lived on Hayward Place in Boston, a short distance from the magazine's offices.

Thomas Niles of Roberts Brothers, Publishers, asked Louisa to write a girls' story, so she started *Little Women* in May 1868. She wrote about her own sisters and their experiences, thinking that "they may prove interesting." May designed illustrations for the book and it was immediately successful when it was published.

Louisa spent the last two months of 1868 writing a sequel to *Little Women*. She described the March girls as they grew up: Meg's happy married life, Jo's struggles as a writer, and Amy's artistic career. Beth's death was described in the chapter "The Valley of the Shadow."

Both volumes of *Little Women* were combined and eventually sold as one book. Its success made Louisa wealthy and famous. At thirty-six, she had done what she had always wanted to do: make her family financially secure.

Mr. Thomas Niles of Roberts Brothers was Louisa's honest, supportive publisher. He worked with her for over twenty years.

May's attempts at illustrating *Little Women* were regarded as not compatible with the writing. Eventually, her drawings were replaced with others.

Many incidents and circumstances from the Alcott girls' lives were used in *Little Women*. Mr. Alcott's favorite book, *The Pilgrim's Progress*, was always used to show his daughters the benefits of virtue, as seen through the experiences of Christian as he travels to the Celestial City. "Playing Pilgrim's Progress" is mentioned in *Little Women*. "What fun it was . . ." says Jo.

The Alcott family's life of generosity and self-sacrifice was infused into *Little Women*. The first chapter, "Playing Pilgrims," begins with these words, vignettes of the characters of Jo, Meg, Beth and Amy.

"Christmas won't be Christmas without any presents," grumbled Jo, lying on the rug.

"It's so dreadful to be poor!" sighed Meg, looking down at her old dress.

"I don't think it's fair for some girls to have plenty of pretty things, and other girls nothing at all," added little Amy, with an injured sniff.

"We've got Father and Mother and each other," said Beth contentedly from her corner.

The *Pickwick Portfolio* described in *Little Women* corresponded to the Alcott family's newspaper, *The Olive Leaf*.

In May's room at Orchard House, homemade theatrical costumes used by the Alcotts are still displayed.

May's drawing represented Louisa as Rudolpho in *Bandit's Bride*. The Alcott interest in theatricals was written into *Little Women*.

"Jo played the male parts to her heart's content, and took immense satisfaction in a pair of russet-colored boots, given her by a friend." —From *Little Women*

Little Women Makes the Alcotts Famous

So closely did readers of *Little Women* identify with the book that soon after its publication, Louisa found herself the subject of interviews and received admiring mail and visitors who were interested in seeing her home and writing locales. Her reaction to her fame is reflected in a reference to her best dress, often worn at many formal occasions in Boston: "People are remarking on how familiar my best black silk has become. I shall either have to get another or go home to Concord. I am going home to Concord."

On a particular occasion in Concord, two visitors were fortunate to find Louisa willing to entertain them. They found her stimulating company. "If eloquence be 'fluent speech,' then was Miss Alcott eloquent," wrote the visitor. She walked with the company to the Concord River, entertaining all the way with stories and lively accounts of her experiences.

"We three left the house and walked towards the banks of the river," recalled Mary Bartol. "Here in a chosen spot had Mr. Alcott raised an arbor . . . to Nature. To this arbor did Miss Alcott lead her friends, who soon turned again to

eager listeners. No watery current could flow and flash more brilliantly than did the stream of speech, and the Concord girl and the Concord River told tales that day never to be forgotten."

May's sketch of the Concord River, a favorite recreation spot for Concord friends and neighbors.

Little Women tells the story of Amy's narrow escape from death when the ice gives way on a skating expedition.

The fame of *Little Women* made the Alcotts of Concord subjects of public interest. Louisa disliked being a celebrity and struggled with that role the rest of her life. She wrote in her journal: "People begin to come and stare at the Alcotts. Reporters haunt the place to look at the authoress, who dodges into the woods . . . and won't even be a very small lion." When curiosity seekers came to the door of Orchard House, Louisa often posed as a servant when she answered. Her family thought she should be more accommodating to those interested in her books, but Louisa claimed her only duty was to write them.

Orchard House.

Little Women brought so much mail from admirers that Louisa sometimes gave it to May or Anna to answer. In 1871 Anna wrote to two Vassar College girls who loved the book. She explained some of the background of the Alcott-March characters: "Jo and Beth and Amy are all drawn from life and entirely truthful pictures of three dear sisters who played and worked, loved and sorrowed with me so many years ago. Jo always admired poor plain Annie and when she came to put her into the story she beautified her to suit the occasion, saying 'Dear me, we must have one beauty in the book,' and so Meg with the big mouth and homely nose shines forth quite a darling and no doubt all the 'Little Women' who read of her admire her just as loving old Jo does . . ."

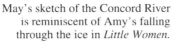

May's sketch of the Concord River
is reminiscent of Amy's falling
through the ice in *Little Women*.

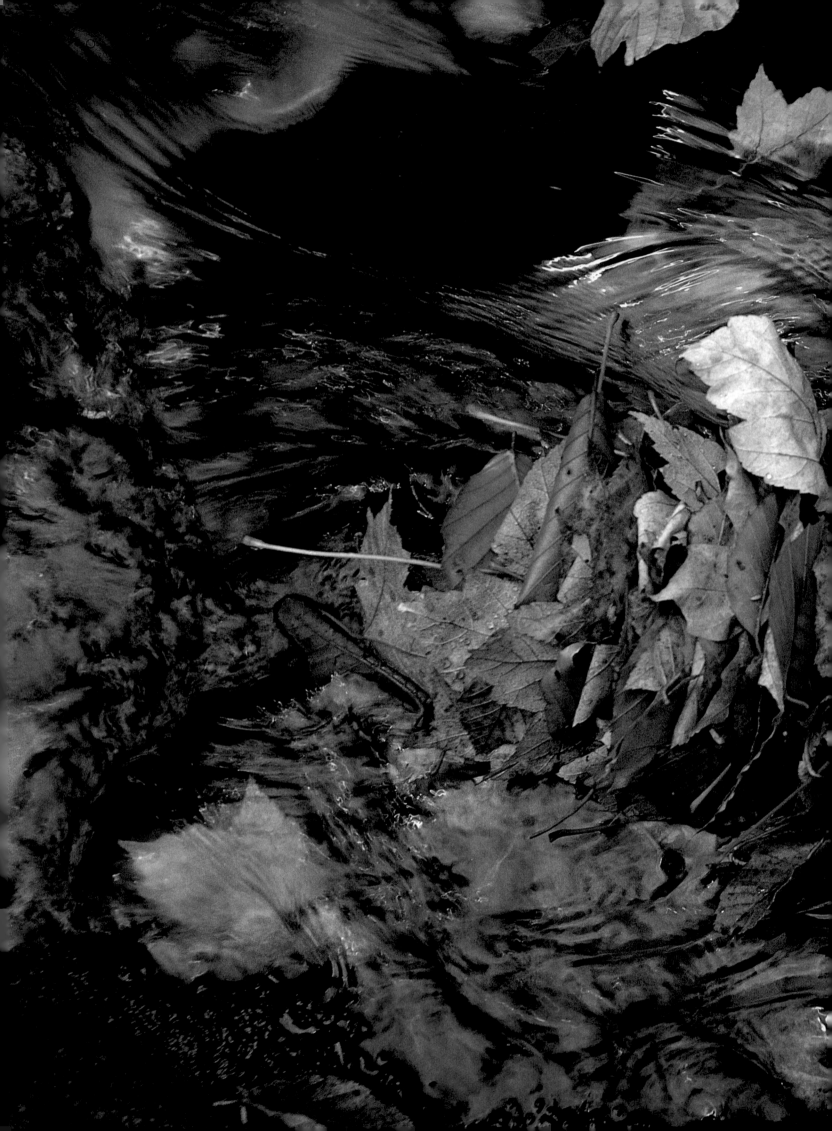

"Life always was a puzzle to me. . . ." —Louisa May Alcott

Little Women Illustrated by Norman Rockwell

Since its first publication, the scenes in *Little Women* have been depicted by many illustrators in dozens of styles. Norman Rockwell (1894–1978), a master at portraying historical settings, created illustrations for a serial entitled "The Most Beloved American Author," which appeared during 1938 in the *Woman's Home Companion*.

"She did not think herself a genius by any means; but when the writing fit came on, she gave herself up to it with entire abandon, and led a blissful life, unconscious of want, care or bad weather, while she sat safe and happy in an imaginary world . . ." —From *Little Women*

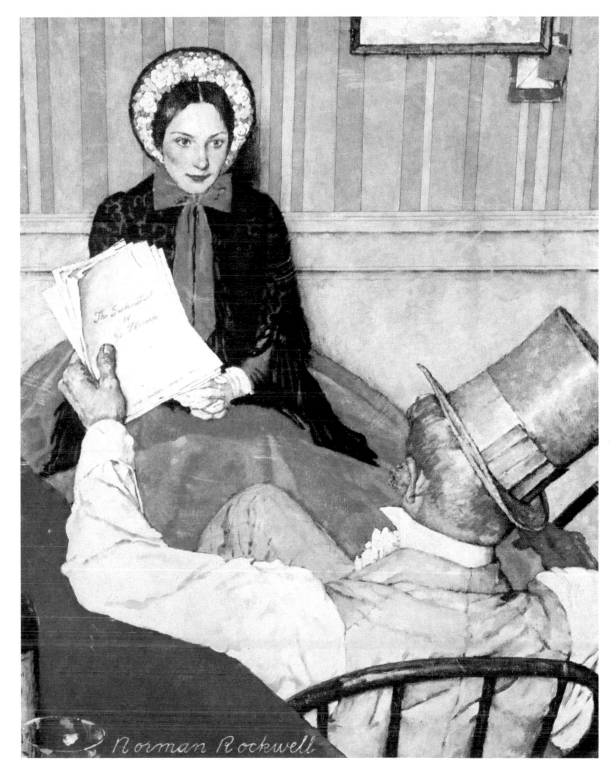

Norman Rockwell

"People want to be amused, not preached at, you know," said
Mr. Dashwood of the *Weekly Volcano,* as he accepted Jo's first
story. "Morals don't sell nowadays." —From *Little Women*

Chap VII.
"Our foreign Correspondent."
—
London Aug

Dearest People,

Here I really sit at the front window
of the Bath Hotel Piccadilly. Its not a
fashionable place but Uncle stopped here
years ago & wont go any where else; however
we dont mean to stop here long so its no
great matter. Oh, if I could begin to tell
you how I enjoy it all! I never can, so
Ill give you bits out of my journal, for
I've done nothing but stare, sketch &
scribble since I started.

I sent you a line from Halifax when
I felt pretty miserable, but after that
I got on delightfully, seldom ill, on deck
all day, with plenty of pleasant people to
amuse me. Every one was very kind, especially the gentlemen. Dont laugh, Jo,
I didn't flirt, & one really does need
gentlemen to hold on by, or to wait upon
one, & they have nothing else to do so its
a mercy to make them useful, otherwise they
would smoke themselves to death.
Aunt & Flo were poorly all the way

A page from the original manuscript of
Little Women describes Amy's tour of
Europe with old Aunt March.

Louisa often became restless in Concord. Although her solicitous mother and her talkative father meant well, their ministrations sometimes interrupted Louisa's writing sessions. Frequent visits from Anna and her sons lured Louisa away from her desk. "My little nephew, Annie's son, is calling 'Aunty Wee-wee' to come and take him for his daily constitutional and the young lord of the house must be obeyed," she noted in a letter to a friend.

Just as Jo of *Little Women* did, Louisa left the family circle for writing stints. Periodically Louisa moved to Boston to rest and concentrate on her expanding literary career.

In her earlier years she could fall into periods of intense writing that she called a "vortex." After her serious Civil War illness her health sometimes prevented her from, as she said, "writing hard." Sometimes her enormous imagination and drive were outstripped by her limited strength.

Though her passion was writing, Louisa was ever mindful of her family. "Don't care much for myself," she said, "as rest is heavenly even with pain; but the family seems so panic stricken and helpless when I break down that I try to keep the mill going."

At the end of 1869 Roberts Brothers sent Louisa a royalty check for $8,500. Her writing had ended the struggling years for the Alcotts. Louisa paid off every family debt she could trace. "I feel that I could die in peace," she wrote. She was able to supply every comfort for her parents at the Orchard House. She helped May in her continuing art education. "My dream is beginning to come true," she said.

Despite requests from her publisher and readers Louisa refused to have Jo marry the romantic Laurie. She favored leaving Jo single, showing a viable alternative to her readers by presenting her alter ego as a successful career woman. Only reluctantly did Louisa finally write in the character of Professor Bhaer as Jo's eventual husband.

Louisa proved that a woman could make a successful career in the predominantly male-dominated field of publishing. Although there were other best selling female authors in the mid-1800s, Louisa was among the first to create a compelling picture of family life.

Louisa May Alcott, author of *Little Women*.

"*Little Women* had been published a year before I knew it," wrote author Mary Bartol. "Absence from New England had kept the book from my view. An acquaintance with it began on shipboard. The day was blue and breezy, the steamer ploughed steadily on her way and several passengers, heretofore confined below had emerged. One of them held a small volume in her hand by Louisa M. Alcott, from which she proceeded to read extracts. How funny they were! O, the adventures of little women . . . How they dared and lost and won! What boatings, what spills, what strandlings, what escapes were theirs!"

An Old-Fashioned Girl, 1870

May and Louisa lived together on Pinckney Street in Boston, moving there in the fall of 1869. Louisa's health was often frail, and she spent time consulting with doctors. She tried a variety of treatments and used opium to sleep. Finally, she decided to try the Victorian alternative of travel in response to ill health.

The Alcott sisters and Alice Bartlett sailed from New York on April 1, 1870; *An Old-Fashioned Girl* was fresh from the printing press. Louisa felt unwell during the ten-day passage, which ended when they docked at Brest, France.

Jessie Willcox Smith was an illustrator for *An Old-Fashioned Girl.*

Louisa's Second Tour of Europe, 1870–1871

May longed to travel and sketch in Europe, and Louisa was glad to make her sister's wish come true. Together with May's friend Alice Bartlett they decided to make a grand tour. The women sewed travel clothing and packed their trunks for departure in April 1870. Louisa gave up her editing duties for *Merry's Museum*. With her large royalty checks appearing regularly, she had no fear of a limited budget.

Alice and May on their European trip.

May's sketch of travel companion Alice.

"Everyone was kind, especially the officers." —From *Little Women*

"We still dawdle along," Louisa wrote to her mother from Vevey. "The food is excellent . . . It is grape time now, and for a few cents we get pounds, on which we feast all day . . . We walk and play as well as any one, and feel so well I ought to do something." It was a long and unaccustomed time for Louisa to remain idle with her pen, but she refused all opportunities to write. She warned her editor, Mr. Niles, not to give her address to anyone. "I don't want young ladies' notes," she wrote firmly. "They can send them to Concord, and I shall get them next year."

Concord was never far from Louisa's thoughts, and she often wrote to each member of her family, sharing the culture and experiences that she encountered in her travels. "I wish the boys [her nephews] could see the funny children here in the little wooden shoes like boats, the girls in blue cloth caps, aprons and shawls, just like the women, and the boys in funny hats and sheepskin jackets," wrote Louisa to her mother while in Morlaix.

Louisa, May, and their travel companion were a congenial trio. They studied French, learned to barter with the local merchants, and enjoyed the sights.

Madame Coste's pension.

One of the first stops on the tour was Morlaix.

May sketched their quarters at Madame Coste's in Dinan.

In June Louisa, May, and Alice stayed at the Hôtel de l'Univers in Tours.

Louisa relented and wrote a poem called "The Lay of the Golden Goose," which described her career and her role as the family provider. When her group settled in for a stay in Switzerland, she read quietly and enjoyed drives in the mountain countryside. May, always more social than her sister, had flirtations, attended parties, and was the belle of the three women. Louisa, sobered by her responsibilities and her role as the source of income for the Alcotts, enjoyed May's carefree attitude, but did not always approve of it.

In June the travelers stopped at the Hotel Metropole in Geneva.

In addition to her artwork, May joined Louisa in taking French lessons. "We *must* speak the language," Louisa told her family, "for it is disgraceful to be so stupid."

As Amy did in *Little Women*, May Alcott practiced and perfected her artistic skills.

May was so productive in her art studies during their tour of Europe that Louisa decided to finance an additional stay for her sister when she returned to America.

May eventually wrote a guide book for young artists.

Some of May's work and her artist's colors.

A birthday letter to her mother dated October 8, 1870, announced, "Here we actually are in the long desired Italy, and find it as lovely as we hoped." Louisa and May wrote home faithfully, and they eagerly anticipated letters in return from their family in Concord. In her journal Louisa recorded that the arrival in Italy signified "a memorable month." She mentioned "heavenly days at the lakes and so to Milan, Parma, Pisa, Bologna and Florence. Disappointed in some things but found Nature always lovely and wonderful, so didn't mind faded pictures, damp rooms and the cold winds of 'sunny Italy.' "

Milan.

Italy was the continuation of May's journey into Europe's art mecca. Louisa was ever mindful that their European trip was an opportunity for her younger sister to improve her skill and saturate her art-loving eyes with the accumulated beauty of centuries. "I mean she shall have a good time," Louisa wrote adamantly to her mother.

Parma.

Florence.

Like many post–Civil War Americans making a grand tour, the Alcott sisters encountered many of their compatriots as they journeyed from place to place. They made many quick friendships, joined newfound friends for excursions, and shopped. In Florence Louisa recorded that they "bought furs." By November 10 they reached Rome. There Louisa had a feeling of déjà vu. "Felt as if I had been there before and knew all about it," she wrote. On November 29 she celebrated her thirty-eighth birthday with a sketch from May and flowers from Alice Bartlett.

Little Men, 1871

While in Rome, Louisa and May were shocked to receive news that Anna's husband John Pratt died on November 29. He was 37. Louisa wrote to Anna, "No born brother was ever dearer and each year I loved and respected and admired him more and more." Louisa's thoughts immediately turned to the support of her sister and her two sons. John Pratt had saved and left a small income for his family, but Louisa was convinced that she should write a book "so that John's death may not leave Anna and her dear boys in want."

Louisa went back to work through the winter in Rome. She wrote *Little Men*, a sequel to *Little Women*, carrying on the March family saga. The setting was Plumfield, a school operated by Jo's German husband, Professor Bhaer. The principles of the school were very much like Bronson Alcott's long-held educational theories.

Louisa felt needed at home, so she sailed for America in May. *Little Men* was published the day she arrived. Her father and her publisher held an advertising sign for the book to welcome her.

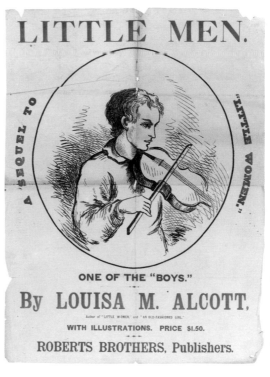

Little Men was subtitled *Life at Plumfield with Jo's Boys.*

Little Men had advance sales of 50,000 copies before it appeared in print.

Anna, Louisa said, mourned John Pratt's death "like a tender turtle dove."

Fred and John Pratt were models for Daisy and Demi in *Little Men*.

Louisa's book *Work* recounted many of her own experiences as a struggling working girl. The chief protagonist, Christie, was Louisa; many of the experiences in the book were also Louisa's. *The Christian Union* paid Louisa $3,000 to serialize the story.

After appearing as a lengthy serial, *Work* appeared in book form in 1873.

Louisa found her mother much aged when she returned from Europe and vowed not to leave her again. After visiting for the summer, she resumed her old pattern of keeping the family comfortable in Concord while she rested and wrote in Boston. She took rooms on Beacon Street and tried to enjoy the city with theater, visiting, and reading. Her publisher brought out a collection of stories titled *Aunt Jo's Scrap Bag* in 1872 and her other books continued to sell well.

During Louisa's first years as a career woman she had been inspired by the preaching of Boston minister Theodore Parker. In *Work*, Parker was the prototype for Mr. Power.

Aunt Jo's Scrap Bag was followed by *Shawl Straps*, which Louisa wrote for *The Independent* about her trip through France.

In 1875 Louisa wrote *Eight Cousins*, but she also devoted time to one of her favorite reforms, women's suffrage. As a tax-paying career women, she found keen injustice in the fact that she could not vote; such was taxation without representation. Both Louisa and her mother signed a petition opposing this practice. Mary Livermore, editor of *Woman's Journal*, came to Concord to speak about women's rights and Louisa sat up all night discussing issues with her. At Mrs. Livermore's suggestion, Louisa attended the Women's Congress in Syracuse, New York. Louisa wished only to be a listener, but was surprised when a crowd of autograph seekers sought her out after the speeches.

Also in 1875 Concord celebrated its centennial. The patriotic atmosphere of Concord brought on what Louisa called a "grand celebration." She was at Orchard House most of the summer, but disliked all the festivities, saying that ninety-two visitors in one month was too many. "Fame is an expensive luxury," she noted. She got a great satisfaction during the centennial when the platform collapsed at the speakers' tent in Concord. No seats had been allocated for women and Louisa believed the collapse was "because they left out the Women's Suffrage Plank."

While Louisa disdained her fame and her fans, Bronson delighted in his increasing success as a traveling speaker. He was very popular in the Middle West and set out each year to tour cities like Dubuque, Iowa; Ann Arbor, Michigan; and Chicago, Illinois. Everywhere he went, Bronson was received with great interest and respect. And he was well paid for his efforts. At long last his ideas won warm appreciation. His status as Louisa's father undoubtedly created an interest in his appearances, and Bronson told his daughter that he was "adored as the grandfather of 'Little Women'."

During Bronson's later years, he published several books, including *Concord Days*, *Table Talk*, and *Tablets*.

The Alcotts always fussed over Bronson when he prepared to leave on tour. Louisa took satisfaction that he could now travel with a trunkful of fine clothes fitting for a venerable philosopher. Bronson liked telling his audiences about Louisa's career and her life, though she asked him not to. He was also asked to discuss Emerson and Thoreau. People seemed interested in everything he said, and Bronson developed the belief that westerners were youthful, energetic, and open to new ideas. "Our Eastern scholars should go West," he declared.

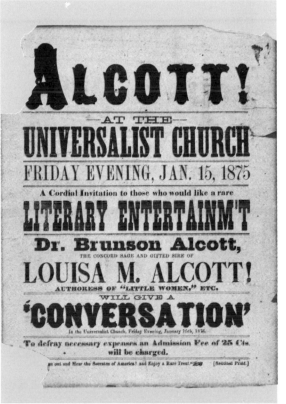

Boston as the Alcotts knew it.

While the western tours enlivened Bronson's life, Louisa was happiest in Boston. In 1874 she settled on Joy Street and later made extended stays at the Bellevue Hotel. She published *Rose in Bloom* in 1876. In 1877, in Roberts Brothers' anonymous "No Name Series," she published *A Modern Mephistopheles*. She enjoyed writing this book for adults, after writing so many works for children.

Louisa was so much in demand that newspapers and magazines constantly asked her for contributions. Roberts Brothers regularly asked her for more novels. In her quiet writing quarters in Boston, Louisa pondered ideas and worked at her craft.

Death of Abba, 1877

When the Thoreau family home in Concord was for sale in 1877, Louisa helped Anna to purchase it. "So she has her wish and is happy," Louisa said.

Abba

"A great warmth seems gone out of my life," Louisa wrote of her mother's death.

Anna

Anna became "house-mother . . . so patient, so thoughtful and tender."

Abba Alcott failed rapidly during 1877. Louisa and Anna nursed their mother faithfully. May had returned to Europe to study art and the family urged her not to return and Marmee forbade it. Sitting by her mother's sickbed during the summer of 1877, Louisa completed *Under the Lilacs*. Her mother asked her to "Stay by, Louy, and help me if I suffer too much."

In November the Alcotts closed Orchard House and moved to Anna's new home in the village. Bronson, Abba, Louisa, and Anna and her two boys enjoyed the spacious house. But Abba was close to death; on November 25, 1877, she died peacefully.

Many of May's original artworks are exhibited today in the preserved Orchard House.

Louisa's traveling bag recalls her many trips, both near and far from Orchard House.

May made a final study trip to Europe in 1877. She worked at her craft in London and Paris and among her artistic friends was the Impressionist, Mary Cassatt. May gained real distinction as a copyist of Joseph Turner, and was able to sell some of her works. One of her still life paintings was accepted by the Paris Salon, which brought her and the family in America great pleasure.

After Marmee's death, May was comforted by her friendship with a Swiss businessman named Ernest Nieriker. On March 22, 1878, they were married in London.

Marriage of May, 1878

Ernest was fifteen years younger than May, but he had a stable income and good prospects in business. He played violin and both he and May appreciated the art world. "My future seems so full of beauty and joy I can think of nothing else," May told the family in Concord.

May's painting of Ernest in their Parisian home.

Louisa May Nieriker was born on November 8, 1879. She became "Lulu" to the family.

Death of May, 1879

May's recovery from childbirth became complicated; she contracted spinal meningitis. For seven weeks May passed in and out of delirium. On December 29, 1879, she died peacefully and was buried at Montrouge cemetery.

A cable was sent to old Mr. Emerson, asking him to tell the Alcotts of May's death. He found Louisa at home and handed her the tragic news.

May had asked her sisters not to mourn her if she died because her last years had been so happy. And to Louisa she gave her little daughter.

"Yours for Reform"

Louisa continued the family tradition of reform. She worked to form a suffrage group in Concord and later was concerned about excessive drinking in the town and was active in the temperance movement. On March 29, 1881, the Concord school committee elections occurred and Louisa cast her vote along with twenty other women. "Women need so much coaxing it is hard work," she complained. But she was proud of her first experience as a voter.

When she could, Louisa participated in charitable and good works. She told stories to prisoners at the Concord State Reformatory, she helped entertain poor city children at Walden Pond, and made a visit to the New England Hospital for Women and Children. Although Louisa often felt unwell, her storytelling helped cheer patients, prisoners, and needy children.

Concord Town Hall, a meeting place familiar to the Alcotts.

Louisa once signed a letter "Yours for reform of all kinds."

The Concord Free Public Library houses Alcott manuscripts and rare material on the literary characters of the town. The Alcotts donated books to the Free Public Library of Concord when it was formed. It was located near Anna's house.

Bronson considered the formation of the School of Philosophy the highlight of his long career. He was proud that Orchard House was the site of an "ideal" school. Women were equally welcome at the summer sessions.

Bronson Alcott's spirit and bust still prevail.

In its simple, woodland surrounding, the school seemed to reflect all the beauty of Transcendental thought. Upward peaks in the building symbolized the human spirit soaring to heights above.

Bronson's long dream of a philosophic school in Concord came true in 1879. Spurred on by western admirers and a one-thousand-dollar gift from a benefactor, the Concord School of Philosophy was established on the grounds of Orchard House. A rustic "hillside chapel" was erected to house courses, lectures, and literary events. On his annual lecture tour, Bronson promoted the enterprise and invited participants. Summer sessions started in July.

The School of Philosophy was a forerunner of the adult education movement in America. Bronson acted as dean, and subjects dear to his heart were discussed: ethics, morals, women, literature, and aesthetics. Bronson was busy and involved in all aspects of the school, even helping to arrange accommodations for out of town guests. "The town swarms with budding philosophers," Louisa noted.

Concord School of Philosophy.

SINGLE TICKET.

Admit the Bearer to ANY SESSION of the Concord Summer School.

A. BRONSON ALCOTT,
Dean of the Faculty.

Concord, Mass., July 1, 1879

Bronson Alcott sits on the steps of his hillside chapel, the School of Philosophy.

While Emerson grew frail and forgetful, Bronson seemed to thrive with old age. In 1881 he embarked on a 5,000-mile tour. Wherever he went, he encouraged visitors to attend the School of Philosophy summer sessions. The school continued to show a profit, as did Bronson's western tours. In May 1882 Anna proudly reported to a friend that "Last winter he lectured for many weeks at the West, bringing home $1,000 for earnings, which was doing well for an old man of 82."

Louisa and Anna were proud of their father, but stayed aloof from his philosophical friends and sessions at the school. They both agreed that after a life of exposure to the intangibles of philosophy, they would settle for the realities of life. Louisa wrote in her journal before the 1882 sessions opened in July that "I arrange flowers, oak branches, etc. and then fly before the reporters come. Father very happy. Westerners arrive, and the town is full of ideal speculators."

Restored and preserved by the Louisa May Alcott Memorial Association, the School of Philosophy carries on Bronson Alcott's intellectual endeavors. Each summer a full program of sessions is offered, covering a wide gamut of subjects.

Life with Lulu

Lulu was cherished by her aunts, her grandfather, and her two cousins, John and Fred.

The Nierikers followed May's wishes and sent Lulu to America to be mothered by her Aunt Louisa. She arrived in September 1880 and immediately the child gave Louisa a distraction from her ill health and grief for May. In her journal Louisa wrote that "My life is absorbed in my baby." The small child's antics gave Louisa new story ideas. The short stories prompted by and told to her niece resulted in volumes called *Lulu's Library.*

During the late 1880s, Louisa took Lulu to Nonquitt, on the Massachusetts shore. She finally purchased a cottage there so that all the Alcotts could enjoy the setting.

Death of Emerson, 1882

On April 27, 1882, Louisa wrote sadly in her journal that "Mr. Emerson died at 9 P.M. suddenly. Our best and greatest American gone. The nearest and dearest friend Father has ever had, and the man who has helped me most by his life, his books, his society." Louisa wrote a tribute to Emerson for the *Youth's Companion*, because she wanted American children to appreciate his greatness.

Bronson continued to be very active during the summer 1882 season of the School of Philosophy. When the sessions closed he worked on a printed edition of lectures given at the school. Suddenly in October, Bronson's creativity and energy were permanently sapped. He suffered a stroke that left him unable to write or speak clearly.

The School of Philosophy continued without Bronson's guidance, but Louisa and Anna agreed that Orchard House should be sold. In 1884 it became the property of Bronson's friend, educator William Torrey Harris.

"I can never tell all he has meant to me," Louisa wrote of Emerson. "His essays on Self-Reliance, Character, Compensation, Love and Friendship helped me to understand myself, and life, and God and Nature. Illustrious and beloved friend, good by!"

Bronson and William T. Harris visit at Orchard House.

Two of Bronson's admirers participated in the School of Philosophy: William T. Harris was first U.S. Commissioner of Education and Elizabeth P. Peabody established the first kindergarten in America in 1860.

Anna's Sons

With Bronson an invalid requiring constant care, Louisa and Anna decided to spend winters in Boston. Louisa rented a stately town house at Number 10 Louisburg Square in 1885. They spent their summers in Concord or at Louisa's cottage in Nonquitt.

John Pratt was adopted by Louisa in 1887, so that he could inherit her book copyrights.

Lulu became Louisa's special responsibility. She is seen on the porch with cousin Fred Pratt.

During the 1880s, Louisa's health was often very poor. She struggled to complete the March family story in *Jo's Boys*, but writing exhausted her. She finally published the book in 1886.

Louisa and Anna took turns caring for Lulu and Bronson. During her summer visits to Nonquitt, Louisa tried to relax. Her friendliness and storytelling made her very popular with children who were vacationing there.

"I need to go away and rest," Louisa wrote.
In 1885 she spent a month in Princeton, Massachusetts.

Jo's Boys was a great literary event when it appeared in 1886. It immediately sold 50,000 copies. One reviewer said, "One takes up this latest book of a dearly loved author with something of a thrill, remembering the delights of *Little Women*. Perhaps Miss Alcott's greatest power lies in her ability to move and influence young minds without the least bit of preaching . . ."

Louisa would not write another novel after *Jo's Boys*. Though she longed to write, she was only able to putter through old manuscripts and arrange short tales for the *Lulu's Library* series and *A Garland for Girls*. "Old ladies come to this twaddle when they can do nothing else," she complained to her publisher.

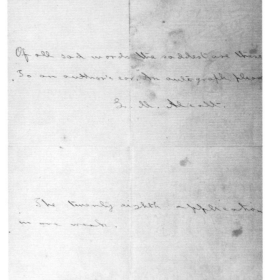

After many requests for autographs, in frustration Louisa wrote, "Of all sad words the saddest are these to an author's ears, 'an autograph please.'"

During the winter of 1888 Louisa took keen interest in the wedding of her nephew Fred Pratt.

Fred married Jessica Cate in February 1888, but Louisa was too ill to attend.

Louisa posed with actor James Murdoch during the summer of 1887. This was the last photograph taken of her.

Louisa in 1885.

Bronson's last years were comfortable, and he was well cared for by his family and nurses, but he never regained his intellectual powers. Speaking, reading, and writing were nearly impossible. Louisa tried to shield him from his admirers and friends, fearing that any excitement would upset him. The family marveled at his beautiful serenity, and though Louisa was sad to see his condition, she wrote, "These painless, peaceful days have a certain sweetness."

Louisa, in a desperate effort to regain her health, left home to live at Dr. Lawrence's convalescent home in Roxbury. She spent many sad, lonely, and painful days separated from her family. But Louisa had always been hopeful, and now she wished for health. Her regimen consisted of a diet of warm milk, and no visitors. Sometimes, when Louisa was able, she slipped into Boston to see her family for brief moments.

Early in March 1888 Louisa drove into Louisburg Square for her last meeting with her father. Louisa knelt next to Bronson's bed and said, "Father, here is your Louy. What are you thinking of as you lie there so happily?"

Bronson pointed upward and replied, "I am going up. Come with me."

"Oh, I wish I could," Louisa replied.

Bronson died on March 4, 1888. Meanwhile Louisa had slipped into a coma, and she followed him on March 6. Her lifelong wish to care for her parents even followed Louisa to Sleepy Hollow Cemetery in Concord. She was buried at the feet of Bronson and Abba. It had been her wish "to support them in death and in life."

There was sadness throughout America when the news spread that the pen of Louisa May Alcott was stilled.

Concord's literati rest in Sleepy Hollow Cemetery.

Anna, Her Boys, and Lulu

With the deaths of her famous sister and father, Anna Alcott Pratt quietly slipped into the role of family matriarch. She presided over the household for her boys and young Lulu, a steady influence and a motherly presence for them all.

In Lulu's tenth year it was decided that she should return to Europe to live with Ernest Nieriker, the father she had never known personally. Anna accompanied Lulu on her journey to Zurich, where they encountered Ernest and his family for the first time. Anna was well-satisfied with the prospects for Lulu's future rearing. She found her brother-in-law "a good man, and I respect him more and more every day."

Louisa May Nieriker Rasim, Lulu.

Back in Concord, Anna, the last of the "little women," followed the familiar routines of daily life in the house Louisa had helped her to buy on Main Street. She lived to see two grandchildren born before her death in 1893.

Anna's sons remained in Concord, dabbling in various pursuits, including the formation of the Concord Motor Car Company in 1906. Together with Lulu they shared the unabated royalties from their aunt's books. Fred Pratt died in 1910; John in 1923.

Lulu spent most of her life in Europe, making occasional visits to relatives in Concord. She married Emil Rasim and had a daughter. Grandchildren recall her as a formidable woman, strong and firm, but with a sense of humor and a dash of the wry Alcott wit. She died in 1975 at the age of ninety-five.

The Alcott Legacy Continues

Still standing under the shady trees along Lexington Road in Concord is the Alcott home, now preserved as a museum. Through the efforts of the Louisa May Alcott Memorial Association, the house still tells its story to thousands of visitors who come from all over the globe to tour it. Orchard House, filled with authentic reminders and cherished memorabilia, basks in the aura of one of America's most unique families.

Louisa May Alcott's writings are read in numerous editions and languages. The timeless quality of her best-known book, *Little Women*, resulted in film versions in 1919, 1933, and 1949, a television adaptation in 1978, and a successful major motion picture from Columbia Studios in 1994, one hundred twenty-six years after its first publication.

Continuing fascination with the life and works of Louisa May Alcott is a phenomenon. Family descendant William F. Kussin observes that "it is the independence of spirit that keeps the Alcott story as fresh today as it was yesterday and insures its place forever."

"Surely joy is the condition of life," wrote the Alcotts' friend Henry David Thoreau. High-principled, joyful living still streams forth from the words and ideals of Louisa May Alcott.

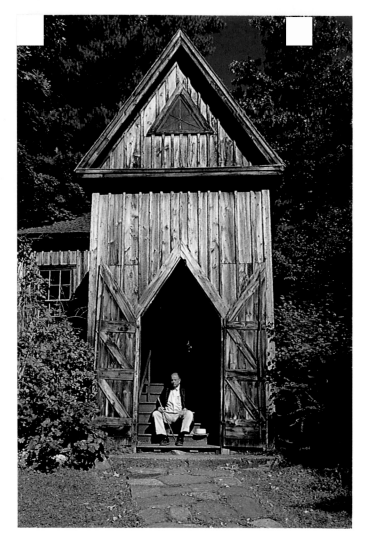

William "Fritz" Kussin, Bronson Alcott's great-grandson.

Founded by Louisa May Alcott's niece, Louisa Pratt Kussin, the Children's Shop has long been a Concord business tradition. Like the timeless Alcott tales, Kussin's shop caters to the young.

In *Walden* Henry Thoreau wrote that his quiet Concord had a single claim to fame, the North Bridge of Revolutionary War renown. Ironically, *Walden*'s publication and the writings of other Concordians helped to transform the New England village in which they lived into a place of literary pilgrimage.

As early as 1872, a seeker of Thoreau's literary haunts came to Concord looking for the Walden Pond house site. She was Mary Newbury Adams of Dubuque, Iowa, a tireless sponsor of philosophical clubs and a promoter of Bronson Alcott's conversations. Mary Adams and Bronson poked around the Walden woods until the latter identified Thoreau's house site. To mark the spot, they piled stones on the site, reviving an ancient tradition of marking significant spots of legend and history.

The admirers of the Concord authors continued to arrive in town to see the sites, despite the fact that by the late 1880s, most of the original group of literati had died. Concord developed as an American literary landmark, a place where great books were born. The former homes of the authors and their grave sites in Sleepy Hollow Cemetery became places of pilgrimage for those who read their words and cherished their thoughts.

Concord's great minds—Emerson, Alcotts, Thoreau, Hawthorne, and others—individualists all, shared the common ground of idealism and commitment to the full development of the individual. Henry David Thoreau's words seemed to summarize each of his circle of friends: "If one advances confidently in the direction of his dreams, and endeavors to live the life which he has imagined, he will meet a success unexpected in common hours."

Thoreau's house site at Walden Pond is commemorated with a rock cairn. Visitors still add stones to the cairn today.

Louisa May Alcott Chronology

Mr. Laurence and Jo.
Scene from *Little Women*.

1799   Amos Bronson Alcott is born in Wolcott, Connecticut.

1800   Abigail May is born in Boston.

1830   Bronson and Abba are married in Boston.

1831   Anna Bronson Alcott is born in Germantown on March 16.

1832   Louisa May Alcott is born in Germantown on November 29.

1834   The Alcotts move to Boston; Bronson forms the Temple School.

1835   Elizabeth Sewall Alcott is born in Boston on June 16.

1839   The Temple School disbands.

1840   The Alcotts move to Concord; Abba May Alcott is born on July 26.

1843   The Alcotts participate in Fruitlands experiment.

1845   The Alcotts occupy Hillside in Concord.

1848   The Alcotts move to Boston.

1851   Louisa's first poem is published in *Peterson's Magazine*.

1852   Anna and Louisa keep a school in Boston.

1853   Louisa teaches.

1855   The Alcotts move to Walpole, New Hampshire.

1858   Elizabeth Alcott dies; the Alcotts move to Orchard House, Concord.

1859   Bronson is appointed superintendent of Concord schools.

1860   Anna and John Pratt are married; Louisa writes *Moods*.

1862   Louisa serves as an army nurse in Washington.

1863   Anna's son, Frederick Alcott Pratt, is born. Louisa writes *Hospital Sketches*.

1864   *Moods* is published.

1865   Anna's son, John Sewall Pratt, is born; Louisa travels in Europe.

1867   Louisa becomes an editor of *Merry's Museum*.

1868 *Little Women* is published.

1870 *An Old-Fashioned Girl* is published; Louisa and May travel in Europe; John Pratt dies.

1871 *Little Men* is published; Louisa returns to Concord.

1873 *Work* is published.

1875 *Eight Cousins* is published.

1876 *Rose in Bloom* is published; May leaves to study art in Europe.

1877 *A Modern Mephistopheles* is published; the Alcotts move to Anna's new home in Concord, where Abba dies on November 25.

1878 *Under the Lilacs* is published; May and Ernest Nieriker are married in London.

1879 May Alcott Nieriker dies in Paris on December 29.

1880 May's daughter, Lulu, arrives to live with the Alcotts; *Jack and Jill* is published.

1882 Emerson dies; Bronson suffers a stroke.

1884 The Orchard House is sold; Louisa buys a cottage at Nonquitt.

1886 *Jo's Boys* is published.

1887 Louisa adopts her nephew John Pratt Alcott.

1888 Bronson Alcott dies on March 4; Louisa Alcott dies on March 6.

1889 Lulu returns to Europe.

1893 Anna Alcott Pratt dies on July 17.

1910 Louisa's nephew Frederick Pratt dies.

1911 Louisa May Alcott Memorial Association is formed to preserve Orchard House.

1923 Louisa's nephew John Pratt Alcott dies.

1975 Louisa's niece, Louisa May Nieriker Rasim, dies.

1994 *Little Women* is released as a major motion picture.

"Jo stooped down and kissed her Friedrich under the umbrella."
—From *Little Women*

Map of the World of Louisa May Alcott

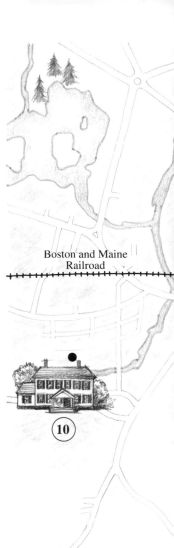

Boston and Maine Railroad

(10)

Walpole, New Hampshire
Home of the Alcotts, 1855–1856.

Wolcott, Connecticut
Birthplace of Amos Bronson Alcott.

New York, New York
Louisa Alcott made visits here.

Syracuse, New York
The Alcott girls made extended visits
and did teaching stints here.

Germantown, Pennsylvania
Birthplace of Louisa May Alcott.

Washington, D.C.
Louisa served as a Civil War nurse here in 1862.

Boston, Massachusetts
A frequent home for the Alcotts.

Lexington, Massachusetts
In 1755, with opening shots fired at Lexington,
Americans engaged with the British in the first battle
of the Revolutionary War.

Concord, Massachusetts
The longtime home of the Alcotts
and other authors of the era.

Harvard, Massachusetts
Fruitlands is located nearby.

Still River, Massachusetts
After their Fruitlands fiasco,
the Alcotts lived here.

Princeton
Louisa spent the summers of 1886
and 1887 here.

Wachusett Mountain
A familiar sight while living at
Fruitlands.

Nonquitt
Location of the Alcott summer
cottage during the 1880s.

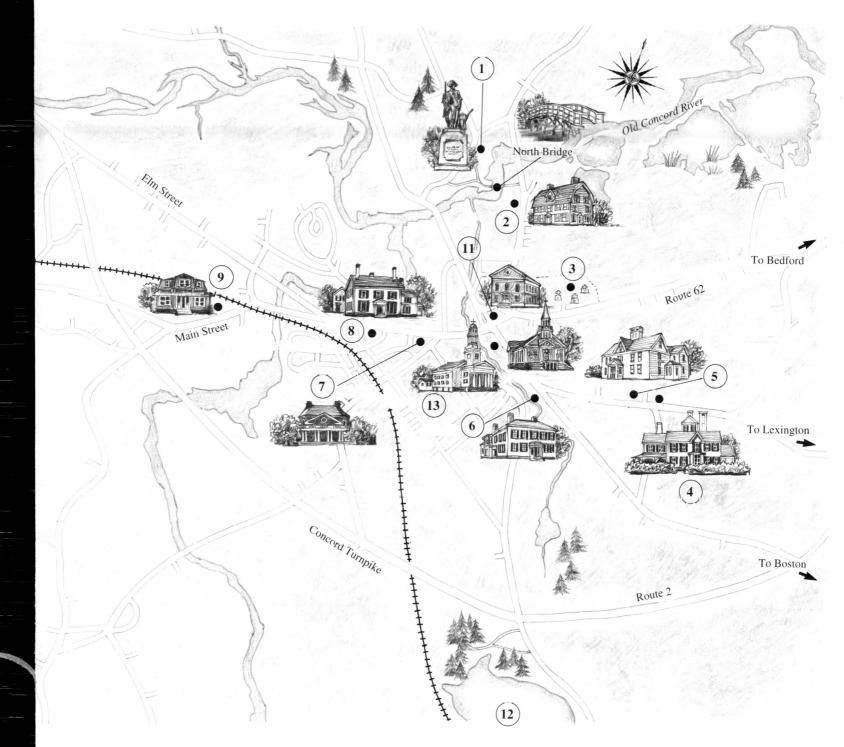

Historic Concord

1 Minuteman National Historical Park and Old North Bridge
2 The Old Manse
3 Sleepy Hollow Cemetery
4 The Wayside, formerly Hillside
5 Orchard House*
6 Emerson House
7 Concord Free Public Library
8 Thoreau-Alcott House (not open to the public)
9 The Dove Cote (not open to the public)
10 Original Thoreau School (not open to the public)
11 Sanborn School (not open to the public)
12 Walden Pond
13 First Parish Church (Unitarian)

*Like most of Concord's historic sites, Orchard House is open to visitors in season.
For information about hours and dates and to join "Friends of the Alcotts," write:
Louisa May Alcott Memorial Association, Box 343, Concord, MA 01742.

Acknowledgments

The idea for this book originated in Japan, when professional translator Yumiko Taniguchi first recognized interest in her country concerning the Alcotts and the Transcendental era. Her formative plans for the book were enhanced through correspondence with the eminent Alcott historian, Madeline Stern. The book was first published in 1992 by the Kyuryudo Art Publishing Company, under the direction of Ryutaro Adachi.

To compile this largely visual documentary of the Alcotts and their times, it was necessary to enlist the help of the organizations and individuals who actively guard and promote the archives and artifacts of the Alcotts. In Concord, the Louisa May Alcott Memorial Association, the Minuteman National Historical Park, and the Concord Free Public Library were of great assistance. Nearby, in Harvard, the Fruitlands Museum was helpful. Research was conducted at the Houghton Library at Harvard, as well as in Concord's Thoreau Lyceum.

Catherine Rivard and Nancy Joroff of Concord were supportive, and input from William F. Kussin was appreciated. Michael Voss of Wuppertal, Germany, kindly supplied photo research. Anita Clair Fellman of Old Dominion University was a valued critic.

The author wishes to cite the National Endowment for the Humanities and their summer seminar programs for secondary educators. Participation in Dr. Walter Harding's 1984 Concord Seminar on Transcendental writers provided a rich groundwork for this book.